When Food is Family

*a loving approach
to heal eating disorders*

Judy Scheel, PhD, LCSW
Foreword by Kathryn Zerbe, MD

Idyll Arbor, Inc.

39129 264th Ave SE, Enumclaw, WA 98022 (360) 825-7797

Idyll Arbor editor: Thomas M. Blaschko
Cover art: Sandra Swenby
Cover photograph: Andrew Cohen

ISBN: 9781882883882
Printed in the United States of America

Library of Congress Cataloging-in-Publication Data
Scheel, Judy, 1959-
  When food is family / Judy Scheel.
     p. cm.
  Includes bibliographical references.
  ISBN 978-1-882883-88-2 (alk. paper)
  1. Eating disorders--Treatment. 2. Family psychotherapy. I. Title.
  RC552.E18S348 2011
  616.85'26--dc23

                                                        2011016539

For my mother, in whose kitchen I finished up the last of this book in the early morning hours prior to her burial. I trust you are dancing in the heavens, momma.

Contents

Acknowledgement

My family is my food — nourishing, calming, interesting, and fun, and a stabilizing force in my life — the necessary ingredients for a healthy existence. I have had the remarkable fortune of raising two children who gave me the opportunity to restore and, in many ways, create for the first time relationships based on deep trust, empathy, respect, and love. They have encouraged me, and continue to do so, to face my shortcomings, confront my mistakes as a parent, and take responsibility. It is their wisdom and love that continue to guide me every day. My gratitude, Meagan and Ian, are beyond measure. Thank you Michael for raising our children together in a loving, safe, open, and respectful home.

I fantasized, from time to time, about how I would thank my patients and their families when I finally finished writing this book. Their lives and experiences are woven into my core. Their courage to face the challenges that come with recovery is remarkable. My perspective, insight, maturity, and deepening empathy are the gifts they have provided. They continue to teach me about forgiveness and compassion for others and myself. I am grateful for their trust, respect, challenge of me, and their kindness. Watching patients grow and evolve into authentic selves and being part of their familial healing process continues to be a source of gratification. It is my belief that through living an authentic life one can affect the lives of others.

It is impossible to imagine this book without the foundation from which it comes. Cedar Associates, the outpatient group treatment practice that I founded in 1994 and now serve as Executive Director, is a unique environment whose strength and longevity have been because of the integrity of the people who work there. It is my colleagues' talent, skill, clinical expertise, practicing with each other what we preach to our patients, and sound advice to me that maintains the success and reputation of Cedar. Thank you, Kristin Lore, LCSW, Director of Cedar's Mt. Kisco office and Elissa Zelman, Psy.D., Director of Cedar's Scarsdale office. You serve as role models to our patients with eating disorders. Thank you Susan Schrott, LCSW, and Jacqueline Reilly, LMSW, who also have been part of the fabric and integrity of Cedar and my life for many years.

I am extremely grateful to the wider community of eating disorder colleagues and professionals who have known and trusted Cedar Associates over the years. The Renfrew Center, Avalon Hills, Timberline Knolls, The Meadows, and Columbia Presbyterian Hospital have worked with us to provide care to our seriously ill patients and have trusted us in discharging their patients to us. Thank you to the local community of health care providers who have cared for our patients and for whom we have provided treatment over the many years of Cedar's existence. Special thanks to Lisa Bardack, MD, and I. Jill Ratner, MD, and their colleagues at the Mt. Kisco Medical Group, Marcie Schneider, MD of Greenwich Hospital, Ann Engelland, MD, Gayle Augenbaum, MD, Flemming Graae, MD, and Maureen Empfield, MD.

When Food is Family went through several transformations and editorial relationships. As with all relationships, a good fit takes time, sometimes a long time, to find. Thank you Spencer Smith for getting the essence of this book and for your editorial expertise and creative conceptualization. Your editorial efforts are second to none.

Thank you Lyndsey Cohn of Gürze Books for working with me in the earlier stages and for your spontaneous and seemingly effortless naming of *When Food is Family*.

Thank you Tom Blaschko, Idyll Arbor, Inc, publisher of *When Food is Family* for accepting this project and for understanding the role that family members play in eating disorders and why delivering this delicate and vital message can serve to aid in recovery and familial healing.

Psychotherapy is an academic and artistic process. My growth as a therapist continues to strengthen through the relationships I have with patients, colleagues, and those in my life who know me personally. The artists in my life have been as professionally and personally influential as the academic training has been.

Andrew Cohen, artist, photographer, and my friend for more than 30 years has helped me see the visual beauty and depth in the human form beyond the body perfect.

Finally, to you Ken Kelsch, ASC, cinematographer extraordinaire and great cook who feeds me every day and reminds me about the calm that comes with trusting and letting go. Your love and wisdom guide me. I am grateful.

Foreword

A family that has a child or loved one with an eating disorder struggles under enormous strain and with unrelenting worry. Anorexia nervosa, bulimia nervosa, and binge eating disorder take a substantial toll on the individual's quality of living and may threaten life itself.

The normal trajectory of growth and development suddenly stops as the child focuses on body image, dieting, achieving and maintaining an unhealthy weight, or overexercise. Often quite consciously, the child's sense of self-worth or level of self-comfort is now derived from these unhealthy behaviors. When family members become aware of the high mortality statistics associated with these illnesses, which rarely yield to any "quick fix" solution from medical or mental health providers, they understandably begin to wonder if they play a role in what caused the problem and what, if anything, they can do to help. For parents and other primary caretakers who are determined to assist their child on the perplexing and often stormy journey of recovery, Judy Scheel's book is an invaluable asset.

Dr. Scheel is a clinician who has worked in the field of eating disorders for over two decades. As the case examples from individual and family sessions make clear, Dr. Scheel knows the terrain of these disorders thoroughly and understands why it is often difficult for the patient to engage in treatment. She offers expert guidance and practical advice that assist the patient and family members on the road back from an eating disorder.

Her therapeutic exercises (that are actually chock full of important questions to make one pause, reflect, and then carefully answer) offer substantial hope because they empower. The tasks Dr. Scheel advises should be undertaken thoughtfully and with paper and pencil. Although they do not lend themselves to easy answers, those who work at the questions will come away with better knowledge of themselves, their family of origin, their child, and perhaps most importantly, a new confidence that "I can do something about this problem. I can help my child."

It is important for the reader to know at the outset that Dr. Scheel bases her approach to treating eating disorders on Attachment Theory and Therapy, one of the most highly researched and evidence-based forms of psychotherapy in the early 21st Century. Attachment Theory is now being applied to help many different types of mental health issues, and the results are robust.

Begun in England in the 1960s by the psychoanalyst and researcher John Bowlby, who originally studied how an individual is affected by sudden and protracted loss, Attachment Theory expanded to include the work of Mary Main and Mary Ainsworth in the 1970s and 1980s (who clarified normal and disrupted attachment patterns in children) and from the 1990s to the present by Peter Fonagy and Mary Target (who have helped trauma victims through their discoveries about adult attachment patterns and personality development).

Utilizing the strong research base of Attachment Theory and applying its findings to eating disorders is a unique contribution of this book and one that parents will find as beneficial as it is relevant in the effort to build trust and instill confidence in the recovery process of their child.

As a practicing psychiatrist and educator who treats eating disorders, I am often asked the question by a patient, family member, or student, "What are the best available books to assist in the 'real world' treatment of eating disorders? Are there any books that offer guidelines that are accessible, sound, and not 'watered down'?" Dr. Judy Scheel's *When Food is Family* is such a text. I recommend it enthusiastically and will keep it on my bookshelf to suggest to families who come for consultation and treatment.

Kathryn J. Zerbe, MD
Professor of Psychiatry and Training
and Supervising Psychoanalyst, Portland, OR

1
Introduction:
Why Eating Disorders are a Family Affair

Eating disorders are scary, especially for parents and other family members. When you watch your child engaging in a behavior that inhibits her ability to nourish her body and grow, it is terrifying. Standing by, watching her starve herself, binge, purge, or engage in other disordered eating behaviors can make families feel completely powerless.

The problem is complicated even further when the disordered eating behavior begins to take hold of the family and contorts or controls your day-to-day life. As a parent, you may start catering to your child's anorexic behaviors, e.g., fixing special breakfasts based on her demands, because you're afraid if you don't, she won't eat. Or you and your husband may sit staring at each other, unable to speak, as your child spends hours in the bathroom vomiting. All the while your resentment of the situation, each other, and even your ill child silently grows.

If you have picked up this book, I assume you are either a parent or family member of someone who has an eating disorder or you may have an eating disorder yourself. That means these dynamics are all too familiar to you.

Eating disorders are no one's "fault." The person with the disorder doesn't want it (at least, down deep she wishes it didn't exist), and most parents don't raise their children hoping they will develop dysfunctional eating patterns. So, judging yourself or your child is not helpful.

That said, eating disorders affect not just the person who has it, but every member of that person's family because, more often than not, the disorder lives with the family. Eating disorders are often a family affair.

Your family feeds you. Your parents provide you with what you need to help your body grow when you are young. But this is only the most basic way your family feeds you. Your family also nourishes you psychologically and spiritually — feeding you from the well of their own emotional experiences.

When it comes to emotional sustenance, the "bread" you are fed is your parents' language and actions. If their language and actions reflect love, support, empathy, and understanding (even of difficult emotional experiences), a bond is created between you and your parents that forms the foundation of your sense of self-esteem and self-worth throughout your life. Healthy bonds make healthy people. Your family becomes your most nourishing "food."

Sometimes these bonds don't develop properly due to circumstances unique to the individual. Family strife or stressors or a predisposing mental health issue for any member, such as anxiety and moderate to severe depression, weakens the family's capacity to provide support, understanding, and empathy. Sometimes the family is unable to identify and articulate emotions in a positive way or does not know how to communicate appropriately, especially when there are familial conflicts. Sometimes there are serious psychological issues for parents or marital issues that impact their capacity to parent. Sometimes the "fit" between parent and child is not natural from very early on. A climate of misunderstanding, perceived or actual criticism, frustration, and helplessness sets in for both parent and child. Eating disorders can flourish in response to this mismatch of personalities and sensibilities.

Support, understanding, empathy, identifying and expressing emotions, and communication provide the psychological nourishment necessary to support the child in building self-esteem and self-worth. Without the development of these abilities within the family, individuals are left psychologically vulnerable. As a result, the child may grow up with a set of challenges that contribute to a range of psychological and interpersonal issues from mild self-esteem problems to more profound disorders like an eating disorder.

Such issues constitute the basic framework of *attachment theory* — the psychological foundation on which this book, and my professional work, is based. Attachment theory tells us that emotional support, understanding, and acceptance during a child's development provide a foundation of safety and trust in the family, and all of these foster self-esteem and self-worth throughout life. The experience of attachment — of being understood, accepted, and loved for who we are, usually within the context of a family — is critical to our healthy development.

Problems in attachment restrict and erode connection and closeness among family members, particularly between parents and children. Dysfunctional family dynamics and confusing or inappropriate patterns of communication can easily emerge, which can leave a child, particularly one predisposed to an eating disorder, feeling insecure, doubtful, and deeply mistrustful. These factors contribute to the development of an eating disorder.

The unfortunate reality is that *many* individuals with eating disorders lack or struggle with attachment. They often feel doubtful and mistrustful of others and do not grow up in ways that leave them feeling secure with themselves. Often, they do not feel connected or close to the people around them. They do not feel accepted for who they are or feel that they are unacceptable to others. They are often unable to tell you how they feel or identify what is bothering them. For whatever reason, they do not experience the emotional sustenance they need to develop a healthy sense of self-esteem and self-worth. The sad result is that they are unable to experience empathy toward themselves. This ultimately leads to a devalued self-image. Once this self-doubt sets in, their ability to know how they really feel and to trust their own internal cues weakens. They then seek out ways to feel better.

Despite these emotional struggles, their inherent craving for these attachments remains and even grows. They may begin to seek fulfillment, closeness, and comfort through food, body image, and weight obsession. In this way, an eating disorder becomes a metaphor — a symbol of their quest for comfort through food, a totem of their guilt for wanting, needing, feeling, and disagreeing, as evidenced by the self-destructive nature of all eating disorders. They create this relationship/attachment to food because the feeling of connection they crave in their relationships — the attachments they truly seek — feel too complicated. Eventually, eating disorders can develop and may become their relationship of choice because real relationships are problematic at best, deeply damaged at worse. The breakdown or void in familial relationships may set the stage for this dynamic to develop.

What causes eating disorders?

Over the last few decades much research has been done into the development of eating disorders and many answers to these questions have been proposed. Clearly our culture, obsessed with body image and thinness at all costs, impacts our perception about our body: shape, size, and weight. Data show that media profoundly influence our body image, that this starts at a very young age, and that the more negative media influences we are exposed to, the more likely it is we will struggle with body-image issues.

But are the expectations of our society and the influence of media the real reasons girls develop eating disorders? If so, why don't all women have anorexia, bulimia, or binge-eating disorder? We all receive cultural messages about the importance of thinness, but we don't all have eating disorders. There must be other causes of the condition. As important as it is to be aware of and critical of these influences, I would argue that cultural expectations are a catalyst for eating disorders, not a principal cause.

A lot of attention has also been given in recent years to the role that innate personality dispositions, biochemical causes, and genetic factors play in the development of eating disorders. While it's clear that each may play an important role and more research certainly needs to be done, the studies to date are inconclusive. We are learning that inherent nature, the disposition we pop out of the womb bearing, may predispose some individuals down the road toward developing an eating disorder. Clinical expertise and more research will hopefully lead to a greater understanding about the causes of eating disorders resulting in more thorough, integrative approaches to treatment.

Most experts and therapists do agree that eating disorders are accompanied by a range of interpersonal problems. People with eating disorders tend to have difficulties in relationships. Often, therapists see these issues as the result of the eating disorder, not the cause. I have come to a wider view.

In more than twenty years of treating people with eating disorders I have come to believe that, although the causes are complicated, childhood relationships and experiences play a significant role in contributing to the development of eating disorders. Relationships impact the development of self-worth and self-esteem. How caregivers interact with, convey their feelings to, and respond to children and each other, and what children perceive and imagine all impact development and identity. Eating disorders tend to center around families. Everyone I have met with an eating disorder had a variety of family issues prior to the development of the eating disorder. And these issues certainly continued or were exacerbated during the life of the illness. Even though the proverbial deck of cards may be stacked by societal influences or genetic predisposition, how the hand is played in family relationships strongly influences whether or not an eating disorder has a climate in which to take hold and flourish. Disordered family relationships provide a springboard to disordered eating patterns.

In recent years, family and relationships have not been considered essential elements in the development of eating disorders. Prior to that, family members, particularly mothers, were "blamed" for causing their child to get sick. Because of this damning view of parents, we lost a lot of support from the professional mental health community and disenfranchised family members who feared blame and shame. That view is changing, and treatment methods are integrating family therapy, not only as a means to help families learn how to deal with the eating disorder once it has been diagnosed but also to examine the impact relationships have on eating disorders. That is what we will focus on in this book: how relationships impact the development and maintenance of eating disorders.

As difficult as it may be to accept, the existence of your child's dysfunctional behavior suggests that there may be problems in your family dynamics and that attachment has weakened. For some, an eating disorder is a voice representing an adaptation to a difficult or intolerable family situation or family relationship. For others, an eating disorder is the vehicle to express and relieve painful or uncomfortable emotions. If emotion is not experienced and expressed, it does not just disappear. An eating disorder is a way to both experience and express what cannot be tolerated. If the person with the disorder were able to experience, accept, and express her emotions and feel able to seek out comfort and support within her relationships, she would be better able to tolerate her "being." Perhaps then an eating disorder would have less chance to develop. She could soothe herself or reach out to others for soothing rather than needing food as the method to soothe internally what she feels unable to tolerate.

Relationships run into difficulty for *many* reasons. I don't mean to suggest you don't understand your child, but you need to ask yourself if the issues or patterns in your family have made it difficult for your child to feel understood and supported or if her eating disorder may be a way to find a voice for what ails her. If you answered, yes, then there are insights and skills you can learn to provide support and understanding in a way that is most nourishing and meaningful.

The good news is that you can learn those skills and restore attachment in your family. You can begin re-experiencing or experiencing for the first time, deep love, empathy, compassion, and support for each other. By doing so you can set a new stage on which your family can function — a stage that will allow the eating disorder to resolve and the person with the disorder, as well as the family, to heal. I wrote this book to help you achieve that goal.

Who I Am and Why I Wrote This Book

I have been treating people with eating disorders and their families for more than twenty years. I founded an outpatient treatment center for people with eating disorders and a not-for-profit organization for prevention of and education about them. I have also lectured, taught, and written articles on this subject. I advocate for patients, attend conferences, and generally keep myself tuned in to the eating disorder community.

The theories on eating disorders have evolved over time but we still are struggling with many of the same frustrations regarding why recovery rates remain low and recurrence rates remain high. Why can't we effectively treat people with disordered eating and distorted body images?

I believe it is because we are not looking in enough places for answers. We are on some of the right paths — predisposing factors and perhaps genetics (the nature aspects), but how a child is raised and regarded, the messages she receives from caregivers during childhood, the experiences she has in and outside of her family (the nurture aspects) play a role as well. A breakdown in family connection and attachment can contribute to the development of anorexia, bulimia, and binge or compulsive eating. Of course, the complete causes of any eating disorder are complex and no single explanation is likely to be uncovered. What we do know, for sure, is that eating disorders are not created by the desire to be thin, even though that is what the person with the disorder starts out believing. We also know that genetic predispositions toward anxiety and depression, and even personality may play a role. But I believe that focusing on these aspects of how eating disorders evolve limits our ability to examine the relational underpinnings that may cause eating disorders to manifest themselves. In short, we have been seduced by the push toward an overly simplistic view of how these difficulties evolve.

I have come to the view that, first and foremost, eating disorders occur because of disorders of relationship, with others and with oneself. By healing these critical relationships, we see long-term healing for the person with the disorder and their family.

I believe that, aside from our physical health, the strength of our relationships sustains us throughout our lives. When our ability to relate to others and ourselves is damaged, it casts a huge shadow that may eventually turn into an eating disorder or an assortment of other psychological problems.

If this is true — if a disruption in family relationships can set the stage or contribute to an eating disorder — then part of the foundation for recovery must revolve around bringing those relationships into greater harmony. If a lack of attachment has contributed to the eating disorder, then rebuilding the attachment is one of the essential steps on the road to recovery.

My goal in writing this book is to teach you how to do that in your own home. This book is a hands-on, working guide to eating disorder recovery that will help you understand some of the psychological and relational underpinnings of eating disorders and the impact they have on both the person with a disorder and the family. This book will teach you ways to work together to heal, repair, and rebuild positive relationships.

This book is written primarily for parents, guardians, and other family members who have a child with an eating disorder still in the home. By explaining the thinking behind my work and using case histories and step-by-step exercises, I will show you techniques you can use to reestablish and deepen the attachment you have with your children. I will lead you through a process of identifying and healing negative family patterns so that your child no longer has to use food as a substitute for relationships, or as metaphors for her life. She will find other ways to express emotions.

Whether or not the person with the disorder reads the book is a decision you should come to as a family. I would not encourage you to "force" her to read this book. Though it will definitely give her some insight into the nature of her eating disorder, she may not be ready to take that step quite yet.

Be aware that I have provided a few exercises throughout the book that are specifically directed toward the person with the disorder. These exercises are designed to help her connect the existence of her eating disorder with the underlying emotional issues that are driving it. They will help her understand and rebuild attachment with you, just as you are working to rebuild attachment with her.

Look at these exercises as an opportunity to open the doors of communication between you and your child regarding her disordered eating. Ask her if she will do them and share her answers with you. If she refuses, you might try other ways to communicate with her, like sharing your answers to the exercises you do as suggested below. If she accepts your invitation, it's a good sign that she wants to reestablish communication, too. However, it also means you will hear some difficult judgments from her about your parenting methods, your communication style, and other issues she finds problematic in her relationship with you. Part of your work is to learn to be present to these judgments without becoming defensive. I will discuss how to do this in more detail throughout this book.

The book may also be useful for adults who have an eating disorder or family members whose child no longer lives in the home but still has dysfunctional eating patterns. The exercises you find here may help you understand what led to the problem and may help you work through some of your relational issues. However, it has not been designed specifically for that purpose.

This book is not intended as a replacement for therapy. It can be used as a useful resource, reference, and teaching guide during a course of therapy. It will also help those of you who have not yet engaged in therapy to understand the therapeutic process and what will be asked of you, the person with the disorder, and other family members during a course of treatment.

The treatment method detailed in this book is what I believe provides the infrastructure for lasting recovery. The theory and philosophy behind this method is what fuels my thinking and provides the theoretical orientation for Cedar Associates, the treatment center I founded and am Executive Director of. I strongly believe that familial relationships and attachment issues addressed in therapy can strongly impact long-term recovery from an eating disorder.

Having said that, other methods of treatment and intervention are often useful and necessary to create a holistic program for overcoming eating disorders, providing support, enhancement, and practical approaches to recovery. I use a variety of treatment approaches in my work, and my center is particularly noted for its integrative approach. For example, the use of behavioral techniques and helping someone change their distorted thinking, commonly known as cognitive-behavioral therapy (CBT), is a component of the recovery "package." Dialectical Behavioral Therapy (DBT), an approach that integrates CBT with Eastern (Zen) practices and focuses on mindfulness, interpersonal effectiveness, emotion regulation, and distress tolerance, has been gaining momentum in treating individuals with eating disorders and is a treatment approach we utilize at Cedar Associates.

Psycho-education for patients and family members, pertinent exercises and group participation to challenge and reflect back distorted views, and seeking input and recommendations of a nutritionist who specializes in eating disorders are all extremely valuable in recovery. In addition, some patients require medication for treatment of the depression and anxiety that often accompany eating disorders. Psychiatric medication is invaluable in helping some patients with, for instance, ruminating thoughts about food and body, lack of motivation to recover, irritability and agitation, and who have levels of anxiety ranging from fear to panic. For sound and responsible treatment, all patients require the care and attention from a physician who treats the unique medical issues surrounding eating disorders.

I want you to understand that the treatment method I prefer is inclusive rather than exclusive. An integrative approach using the best practices available is usually the most efficient in helping a person overcome the disorder. In this book, I focus on attachment theory, problematic relational issues that set the stage for the development of an eating disorder, and the existence of the disorder as a metaphor for otherwise hampered emotional expression for two important reasons:

1. I believe these issues underlie and impact the disorder, yet they are often ignored or marginalized both in therapy and within the home. I want to reverse this trend.

2. There is no other book currently available that focuses on healing broken attachments and analyzing the emotional underpinnings of the eating disorder in a step-by-step, self-help fashion. My goal in writing this book is to add another dimension to the literature on the topic, in the hopes that it offers readers like you a new perspective on the disorder and thus new hope for healing.

Whether you are in therapy now or using this book as a preliminary self-help treatment, keep in mind that the cornerstone of healing is the ability of the *entire* family to experience empathy and extend that sense of empathy to one another. True and lasting recovery has the opportunity to occur when forgiveness, respect, and the true nourishment of emotional intimacy replace denial, resistance, anger, and blame.

When Food is Family will show you that families can — and must — do more than understand and support a loved one with an eating disorder. It is only through the family working together that *all* family members can recover and heal. I welcome you on our journey together.

Accepting Your Part in the Problem

Through this process you will face difficult truths about how actions and words led to a breakdown of attachment between you and your child. For many parents this is one of the most difficult experiences they will ever have. After all, you love your kids more than anything in the world. I know that. Realizing that you have (albeit inadvertently) lent a hand in the psychological and relational issues that contributed to the development of your child's illness is earthshaking. This is not an easy road to take.

In addition to coming to terms with your own involvement in the disorder, you are also going to have to learn how to cope with some very difficult, negative emotions over the course of your family's recovery.

It is no mystery that people who have difficulty tolerating food also have difficulty tolerating negative emotions. The fear, anxiety, and self-disgust that accompany "fullness" build a metaphor for the inability to deal with difficult emotions like sadness, anger, shame, guilt, or the selfishness many people with eating disorders experience because they have been told they are difficult, different, or the round peg in the familial square hole. Projecting these feelings onto the body by feeling "full" is easier than embracing negativity and conflict inside themselves. Odd and troubling as this may sound, it becomes easier to have an eating disorder than to allow oneself to feel bad. It is "easier" to feel self-disgust because of having eaten "too much" than to feel disgusted by one's being.

A child develops a sense of self-awareness and security when family members are able to identify, discuss, and tolerate *all* their feelings — particularly negative ones. The child gains the ability to experience and integrate these emotions when the family provides a reliable model of how to do that. That means you and your family are going to have to learn a method for "sitting with" your anger, shame, guilt, and hurt. This, too, is a difficult and often painful road to take.

It takes bravery and commitment to walk this path. Yet, by picking up this book, you have already made an important step on your and your child's road to recovery. Admitting that there is a problem, that you need help, and then committing to do whatever it takes to rebuild the attachment between you and your child is the first step to revitalizing the love in your family.

The light at the end of this tunnel is nothing less than a loving and connected family where the eating disorder no longer plagues your child and you are able to feel attached and empathetic toward each other in new and profound ways.

Everyone involved in this process should keep in mind that one of the major goals of recovery is for the person with an eating disorder to experience herself in a more balanced, compassionate, and loving way — to take better care of herself. It's important that the person offer herself empathy and compassion for the pain she's experiencing. It's easy for a person with an eating disorder to lose sight of her pain, to beat herself up, to think she's weak or sick or crazy for having the disorder or, conversely, to feel empowered by the disorder so as to trick herself into believing that her pain does not exist. Keep in mind that the eating disorder is a manifestation of and metaphor for her pain as well as a punishment for her vulnerability or perceived "weakness." The goal should be for the person to accept the full range of emotions she's experiencing instead of getting locked into one of these unhelpful patterns.

Most importantly, everyone in the family needs to remember that recovery is a *process*. You all want her to get better. The only way for that to happen is if the whole family learns to share responsibility for the eating disorder. There will be setbacks along the path. Some days recovery will look like it's miles away and some days it will seem to be around the corner. This is not an easy, quick, or painless process, but it does work as long as you keep working the program and keep developing the attachment, empathy, and love you have for one another.

How to Use This Book

This book is designed to educate you about the nature of eating disorders and provide a step-by-step path to recovery.

In Chapter 2 I explain some of the mechanisms by which eating disorders develop, how a breakdown of family dynamics makes its contribution, how food can become family when attachment fails, how eating disorders function as metaphor, what attachment theory is, and how you can use the concepts of attachment theory to help your child heal from her eating disorder.

Then, in Chapters 3 through 8 I provide a series of step-by-step exercises carefully designed to help you:

- Understand and confront problems in your family.
- Learn a "language of emotions" that will give you the tools you need to express your feeling to one another.
- Rebuild trust or perhaps establish trust in your family for the first time.
- Establish healthy boundaries in your family unit.
- Rebuild connections and develop a deeper attachment with one another.

The exercises will ask you to reflect on your reactions to major themes in each chapter, respond to role-playing situations, and take specific actions that will help change how you, as a family, relate and interact.

Each parent reading this book should write out his or her responses to all of the exercises you find in this book. I'm a big proponent of writing down your answers because, if you've ever kept a diary or journal or have written letters, you know that writing can help you tap into emotions and insights you hadn't anticipated. It enables you to connect deeply with what you think and feel. Taking the time to write out responses to the exercises in this book will allow you to think about and investigate your reactions in a way that "answering the questions in your head" never can.

I also recommend that you come together as a family and discuss your responses to these exercises whenever that's possible. Talking together as a family about your emotional experiences is an essential part of healing. Sharing the exercises will help open up the lines of communication in your family once again.

If the person with an eating disorder is reading and working through this book along with you, then these conversations will likely be a little smoother. If that isn't happening, the exercises I have created for the person should facilitate communication, although the road may be a little rockier. If your child refuses to do the exercises or you choose not to give them to her, I recommend you still open a dialog based on each of the exercises. You may want to explain to your child that you are concerned about some of her behaviors and that you have decided to work on your communication and attachment skills in the hopes of becoming a better, more empathetic parent. I think you might be surprised how positively your child will respond to this.

Though it's likely you will have the urge to plunge right into a family discussion as you go through the exercises, I recommend you resist that urge. Writing out your answers *before* you talk has many advantages. First, you won't have to worry about making responses on the spot to sometimes-difficult questions. Second, you don't have to worry about saying whatever comes to mind — which might not always be the best thing to say. Third, writing out your answers to the questions can deepen and enrich your understanding of the concepts and the resultant conversation will be much more productive.

So you should come to the exercises equipped with a journal and ready to write.

As you write out your answers, try a technique called "freewriting." Here's how you do it:

1. Write quickly without stopping for 20 minutes.
2. Keep your hand moving the whole time.
3. If you don't know what to say, write, "I don't know what to say" until something comes to you.

4. Don't worry about grammar, spelling, punctuation, or how the writing sounds. Just keep writing.

Once you try this technique a few times, I think you'll see that it's a powerful way to work through the issues discussed in the exercises. Keep in mind that it's not the length of the writing or its "quality" that counts. What's important is your ability to tap into what you're feeling. So you really shouldn't worry too much about how your writing looks or sounds, as long as you get in touch with your true emotions.

You may find that you need or want to work through some of the exercises more than once as you move toward recovery. That is absolutely fine. This book is meant to be used as a manual that will assist you on your path. Come back to exercises as often as you need, re-read sections to refresh your memory of the concepts found there, and keep referring to the book as your attachment to one another grows.

While a rigorous schedule probably isn't useful, it is crucial that you work through this book and the exercises and meet to discuss them on a regular basis — perhaps weekly. If you have too much time between sessions, you won't experience the same kind of progress as you will if you work through the book at a consistent pace.

That's about all you need to know as you head into Chapter 2 and begin your work to help your family heal. I hope what you have read so far resonates with you. But more than that I hope you, your loved one with an eating disorder, and your family can use the steps in this book to deepen your love and create an environment where a disordered relationship with food is no longer necessary.

When to Seek Medical Help

Since eating disorders have the potential to develop into very serious medical conditions, every person with an eating disorder should seek medical care. The health care provider will then determine the frequency of visits, timing of tests, and medical stability. Communication among all members of the treatment team, which can include a therapist, nutritionist, psychiatrist, and medical practitioner, is necessary in treating eating disorders. Communication among providers is not only extremely helpful in understanding and administering care based on the particular needs of the patient; it is also a way to communicate to the family the seriousness of the condition and remind them that they are not alone in the process. For more information on medical issues and treatment, please refer to the Appendix and Resource section at the end of this book.

Gender and Usage

The personal pronoun *she* is used predominantly throughout this book. This is done because the incidence of eating disorders for women versus men is 9 to 1. The program also can be used for men who have eating disorders.

Stories and Illustrations

The stories in this book are taken from years of practice and are not based on any one individual or family. All of the names, events, and circumstances have been changed to protect the families, but the situations described reflect accurately the interactions between eating disorders and relationships.

2
When Food Becomes Family:
Why Broken Attachments Underlie Eating Disorders

An eating disorder is a voice — a language the person with an eating disorder uses to say with her body what she can't say in words. The symptoms of the eating disorder represent how she feels and what is going on in her life. And food itself becomes a metaphor — often a metaphor for control of a life that feels despairing, helpless, and alone.

But how and why does this happen? Why would a young person resort to expressing her feelings using dangerous behaviors like starving herself, bingeing, purging, or eating compulsively? What could be so out of balance in her life that food becomes the way she attempts to control her reality? What messages do these behaviors communicate? And what causes these disordered eating patterns in the first place?

When you are a child, the way your family relates to one another forms your perspective about the safety and reliability of relationships in general. If your parents treat you with respect and care, you will develop an understanding of relationships that are built on these feelings. If they provide you guidance without attempting to control, manipulate, or judge you, you will learn to trust them and yourself. If they listen to your thoughts and feelings with openness, empathy, and compassion, self-doubts will diminish and you will have a stronger sense of self-worth and self-esteem.

In short, you will develop a strong and healthy *attachment* to your parents. Attachment refers to the emotional bond you develop to the people in your life. This idea is the core concept that informs both my work as a therapist and the contents of this book — *attachment theory*.

The basic premise of attachment theory is that emotional attachments are a fundamental human need. Our childhood attachments form the basis for our emotional and social growth. However, our need for attachments does not end there. Empathy, compassion, and love are not only necessary in childhood but throughout our lives. Once we establish healthy connections with our family, we can more easily establish healthy connections with ourselves and others.

Problems arise when attachments in the family are damaged or non-existent. If parents lack the language necessary to deal with emotions; if there is little room for the free and healthy expression of feelings, especially difficult feelings, within the family unit; if trust, respect, empathy, and compassion are not readily available in the household; then children are trained to bury their emotions. Attachments are broken, and the child's healthy emotional development is less likely.

Sometimes these deformed attachments are experienced as a feeling of disconnection from family members. In other cases the family becomes enmeshed and the entire household is "breathing the same air." Children in these circumstances often feel "different" or "difficult." They have a hard time attaching to something as basic and necessary as their own identity, as they feel consumed by their family's voice and confused or guilty about their own. But their buried feelings and lost sense of identity don't just disappear. They go somewhere. They yearn to be expressed. In the absence of healthier and more appropriate models of emotional expression, eating disorders provide a solution — a language the child uses to communicate her anger, dismay, frustration, fear, and pain.

In this sense, an eating disorder is a metaphor — a symbol for all that is unable to be experienced emotionally and expressed verbally by the person with an eating disorder. The eating disorder is the voice of all the relational issues and conflicts that the individual is unable to identify and express. The eating disorder speaks for her.

Feelings find a way to be expressed no matter how much we want to deny them. Even if we do not know how we feel on a conscious level, we are still feeling and reacting to people and situations deep within ourselves. The eating disorder becomes a way to experience emotions through the physical symptoms and eating behaviors — by starving, purging, or overeating.

If a family has not been able to develop an emotional language, lacks empathy, or does not have the ability to support and understand their child, that doesn't mean the child's need for these things disappears. The child still has feelings and still needs understanding. Her self-worth and self-concept is dependent upon feeling understood.

In fact, a person who has an eating disorder is often *starved* for feelings of closeness, support, and understanding, because she has learned to deny her emotional needs. Or, conversely, she feels that her needs are "too much," that she herself is "too much," and her demands are "too much." As a result, she feels guilty for wanting and needing. She needs her family's support, but she sometimes become highly ambivalent, confused, and at times even threatened by it. In such a situation, her emotional needs — this hunger — turns toward food, a safer and more reliable friend than family — and in many cases, the only consistent friend she will have while her disorder is active. She trusts in food's availability and accessibility in a way similar to a healthy person's trust in the comfort and safety of relationships. In this way, food becomes her family.

What You Can Do When Food Has Become Family

Your child has an eating disorder. If she didn't, you wouldn't be reading this book. The eating disorder itself may show up in any number of ways — eating disorders come in as many shapes and sizes as people do. But there are often fundamental and consistent reasons why people develop eating disorders and the emotional needs that drive them are the same. Your child craves a bond with you; she needs your love, understanding, empathy, support, and trust. For whatever reasons, these attachment needs are not being met in your family. Her eating disorder may have developed in place of much-needed attachment.

I know that can be a hard pill to swallow. One of the most difficult realities that parents of children with eating disorders face is that they helped cause the disorder. That means they have a responsibility to help their child overcome it.

That doesn't mean the eating disorder is the parent's "fault." I don't believe it is. You may have attachment problems for many reasons — some of which could be beyond your control. Perhaps you were raised in a household with weak attachments, so you never learned the emotional language needed to properly nourish your child emotionally. Maybe you're a single parent who works eighty-hour weeks just to keep your family afloat financially and you just haven't had the time to develop deep connections with your kids. It could be that you have problems in your marriage that are affecting your familial ties, or you may even have difficult relationships with extended family members that make it difficult to be fully present for your children and their needs. Perhaps you have your own issues regarding weight, body image, and food that have negatively influenced how you respond to your child regarding these issues, or perhaps you have an untreated eating disorder yourself.

Whatever the reason, it is possible that your child has adopted an eating disorder in place of the nourishing emotional attachments she needs with you. That means for her to fully overcome the disorder those bonds are going to have to be rebuilt or created for the first time.

The good news is that this can be done, and that's what this book is about. I will guide you through a series of step-by-step exercises that will help you develop a "language of emotions" and other skills you need to reestablish an attachment with your child. When you rebuild your emotional ties with your child using the steps in this book, it will be one of the most gratifying experiences of your life. I have never known any family who regretted growing closer to one another.

The bad news is that it won't be easy. It's going to take commitment. It's going to take work. And, most of all, it's going to take an investment in developing so deep an understanding of your child and her eating disorder that she can actually feel understood by you. This is called empathy. Expressing empathy is a key component of this book and a powerful influence in recovery for your child.

You might not be ready to make a commitment yet, but let's start the process to show you how it's done. The first step on your journey to recovery is to understand a little bit more about what I mean when I say the word "attachment."

Most psychological theories today agree that many factors — biological, environmental, cultural, and religious — influence the development of children. At the core of healthy development, however, remains the initial bonding experience with parents or primary caregivers. Understanding the nature and value of these bonds and learning ways to improve them if they are healthy, or repair them if they aren't, is essentially what attachment theory — and this book — is all about.

I believe attachment theory is one of the most dynamic models for treating eating disorders and the healthiest model for raising children. Developing an understanding of it now will not only deepen your experience with the concepts and exercises in this book, but will also lay the groundwork for a lifetime of stronger attachments.

Attachment Theory: An Overview

Attachment theory is based on the belief that bonding early in childhood affects one's self-esteem and relationships throughout life. These bonds, or *attachments,* not only give children the emotional stability needed to weather the storms of life, they also provide a basis for handling their emotions which, as we all know, are sometimes difficult to cope with. Family attachments provide a model on which other relationships will be founded for the rest of their lives. If a child feels safe in her attachment, then she feels safe to explore her world — both her internal world of fantasies, dreams, wishes, wants, and intuition, and her external world of life experiences and interpersonal relationships.

Most of us can remember snuggling into a parent's or grandparent's arms, being read a bedtime story, being tucked in and given a goodnight kiss. These are examples of attachment behaviors. The reason children seek these attachments has been debated in psychological circles for more than a century. When John Bowlby, the founder of attachment theory, trained to be a psychoanalyst, two schools of psychological thought prevailed. On one side of the argument were those influenced by Sigmund Freud. The other side would eventually be comprised of Bowlby himself as well as people like D.W. Winnicott, W.R.D. Fairbairn, and Margaret Mahler.

Psychoanalysts influenced by Freud believed that children seek attachment not to feel connected, but in order to not feel anxious. For example, if a child didn't receive the level of affection from her parent that she desired or if she otherwise wasn't getting her needs met, she would create an "attachment" to overcome the dread that might arise. This bond would soothe the child's anxious mind and would create an emotional tether that would help insure she got what she wanted from her parents in the future.

While Bowlby initially agreed, he quickly began to realize that this model of attachment had serious shortcomings. Freud's theories are founded upon the belief that human beings are driven by aggressive and pleasure-seeking instincts and that they seek socially acceptable ways to express and discharge these energies, or "drives" as Freud called them. Going back to the example above, when the child didn't get what she wanted, she sought an attachment that would not only salve her painful anxiety but would also help her get what she desired in the future. (It's interesting to note that Freud himself seemed to relent on this position in his later writing and began to consider the possibility that feeling close to others was primary, not just a vehicle for getting one's needs met.)

Bowlby began to ask questions: What if human beings aren't driven by the need to gratify "instinctive impulses?" What if they aren't seeking ways to discharge their drives? What if attachment is fundamental to human nature, not the outcome of an anxious mind? And what would happen to children who didn't have this fundamental need met? What would happen if a child didn't have an experience of bonding and attachment with a caring adult figure?

To begin answering some of these questions, Bowlby's early work focused on children separated from parents through death, divorce, or illness. In a key finding, he studied juvenile delinquents who were raised in institutions from the age of seven months. He found that they were impaired in motor and language development and had difficulty forming stable relationships. They also experienced intense feelings of pain, sadness, and anguish that did not diminish in adulthood. This led Bowlby to believe that a child who was separated from her caregivers for a prolonged period during the first five years of her life would develop character problems later on.

If this were the case, i.e. if prolonged separation from a caregiver led to problems with character development, it would appear that attachment is not created to satisfy instinctive, pleasurable, or aggressive needs or impulses but is rather an inherent psychological need of its own. It is fundamental to the healthy and natural development of human beings and their social relationships.

This is the belief that Bowlby and other post-Freudians adopted. These "relational theorists" did not believe as Freud did that aggressive responses like anger were solely innate. They believed also that anger and other emotional states were a consequence of an interpersonal interaction — a child experiences anger when she is frustrated, provoked, or not gratified, i.e., when she does not have a healthy attachment with the people in her life.

Although the ideas put forth by each relational theorist differed slightly, their views were the same on one central point — attachment to a caregiver is the cornerstone of a child's sense of stability, safety, and self-esteem. Two main precepts form the core of Bowlby's work:

1. The bond between parents and children is extremely important.
2. Children need a secure and stable environment that supports the understanding that separation and loss are inevitable consequences of attachment.

The first is an obvious outcome of the concept that attachment is a fundamental human need. If it is, then it's obvious that the bond between parent and child (or caretaker and child) is of the utmost importance. The second point is a little less clear on the surface. Why would it be necessary to present a stable environment that supports the understanding that separation and loss is inevitable?

In a moment, I will discuss why Bowlby's rationale for focusing on loss and separation as a necessity for healthy psychological development is so critical. But before we get to that, let's do our first exercise.

Exercise: Attachment in Your Family

This exercise is designed to give you a sense of how attached you are to the members of your family. It will give you an idea about your own bonding experiences and feelings of connection. Take out your journal and respond to the following questions. Remember to be as honest and thorough as possible. Once you have answered the questions, sit down and discuss them with your family members.

- How would you describe the closeness of the relationships in your family? Are they as close as you would like? Why or why not?
- How does your family demonstrate that they are close to each other? In spoken words? Or is closeness shown through actions or behavior? Please describe.
- How do family members communicate with each other? How would you describe the way they communicate?
- How would you describe your style of communicating with members of your family? Do you feel you are heard? Why or why not?
- What ways of communicating or behaving keep your family from feeling connected to each other?
- How is anger expressed in your family?
- Is expressing anger in your family seen as positive or negative? Do people withhold their anger or express it? Is everyone expected to get along all the time? Or is conflict considered normal?
- Is it easier to be angry in your family or is it easier to express feelings of hurt, sadness, or fear?
- Does your own anger serve to push people away? How?
- Is there too much closeness in the family? Is everyone expected to think alike, feel alike, and not act differently or independently? Or are people allowed to be different?

> - Is there too much distance and separation in your family? Is there a sense that you don't know how others are feeling or what is important to each family member?
> - How has the eating disorder affected the closeness in your family?

The Importance of Accepting Painful Emotions

Whether we are willing to face it or not, the truth is that we all experience pain. We experience loss and separation as well. And often we experience those emotions because of or along with the people we love most — those with whom we share attachments. The pain itself is often an outcome of love. After all, the people you love most are the ones you are saddest to lose. The relationships with the deepest bonds are where the greatest capacity for pain, anguish, and anger exist.

Given this reality, you would think that as a society we would have developed ways to handle painful emotional experiences — especially among our family and friends. Yet often this isn't the case. In most family settings positive emotions like love, happiness, and peace are far more acceptable than negative emotions. Consider your answers to the questions in the exercise above. Do they reflect this dynamic in your family?

In one way this makes perfect sense. It's much easier to accept positive emotions than negative ones. That's natural. And yet it's exactly why we should focus on developing tools to cope with negative emotional experiences. Since they are so much harder to deal with, it makes sense for us to work on creating an environment where we and our children can deal with pain, loss, and separation.

I have seen the difficulty many families have with accepting and integrating the "bad" emotions of people with eating disorders. I suspect you have heard your child proclaim that only "good" food is acceptable. Typically, "good" food is low in calories with little or no fat. Just as, in some households, emotions are strictly divided into those that are "good" and those that are "bad," many people with an eating disorder make the same distinctions between foods. Here the use of "good" versus "bad" food is a clear example of how symptoms and food are used as metaphors to convey emotions, thoughts, and relationships that may be difficult or negative. Just as recovery requires eating a full range of foods, including food with fat, carbohydrates, and sugar, it also involves the integration of all emotions. We need to deal with both those that are "positive" and those that are "negative."

This integration of all human emotions was a foundational element in Bowlby's work, and I believe it is essential in the treatment of eating disorders. When the going gets tough, the tough don't get going — unless they have support. If emotional attachment is an inherent human need, then why do we, as a culture, so often push our children toward premature emotional independence at times when they need us most? Time after time, we fail to encourage our children to be emotionally bonded to us, and this happens most often when they are facing difficult emotional experiences.

Rather than sitting down and talking with our kids, we take a "fix-it" approach when they confront us with perplexing or upsetting feelings. Our motives are good. We don't want our kids to experience pain, and what pain they do experience we want to salve as quickly and completely as possible. So we tell them, "There's nothing to be afraid of," or "Don't worry, it's all right," or "There's no reason to be so angry, let it go." We encourage them to "move along" to the next activity. We teach them to push past the pain.

While these seem like well-meaning attempts to minimize and soothe a child's discomfort, they usually fail because they do not address the underlying issue at hand. They do not take into consideration how the child is feeling and what she needs from her parents. They tend to discount the child's emotional needs and teach her to keep her feelings "inside" or deny them entirely.

This is a failure of attachment. Whenever a child expresses a need or a fear, it's an opportunity for a parent to participate in bonding — the food of emotional well-being. By making an intellectual response or by minimizing the child's emotions, we foster a premature independence that leaves children incapable of experiencing their feelings fully or understanding the motivations behind their behavior. We encourage thinking almost to the exclusion of feeling. Yet our thinking and the subsequent decisions need to be guided by our feelings. Without this emotional infrastructure we are ill equipped for mature independence. That is, we are left responding to situations as we think we ought to rather than being guided by how we really feel.

Interestingly, we tend to encourage dependency of a different sort — one that leaves our children no more prepared to face adult challenges than our denial of difficult emotions. We buy them stuff. In a culture where "more is better," our "instinct" is to meet our children's needs with our purchasing power. Whether it's the latest technological gadget or a new wardrobe, when the going gets tough, we pull out our credit cards, give them what they want, and believe that then our children will feel happy and fulfilled.

But material gratification does not provide lasting comfort and cannot satisfy children emotionally. In fact, it only serves as another way for them to deny and bury their difficult feelings. We are raising children who do not know how to deal with frustration or embrace delayed gratification.

Rather than encouraging a healthy emotional dependence on us, so that they can learn to identify, experience, and accept their emotions (whatever they may be), we teach our children to distance themselves from their emotional world: to bury feelings or, even worse, deny their existence. At the same time, we give them a false sense of dependency by providing comfort with the latest toy or apparel. We teach them nothing of dealing with the pain, loss, or separation that is part of life.

The consequence is children who are easily frustrated, who need constant and varied stimulation, and, most alarmingly of all, who begin to determine their self-worth by cultural norms, e.g., how much more or less they have than someone else. By learning to lean so heavily on cultural dictates for self-worth, many begin to obsess about beauty as a way to make themselves feel confident and accepted. This only serves to further encourage eating disorders.

Though we are hard-wired to experience feelings, we need help in putting names to these feelings. Children learn language by being spoken to — they learn to identify and tolerate their emotions when a caregiver tunes in, puts a label to their experience, and allows the child to sit with her emotions so that she can learn to name and express them appropriately.

This attachment is the foundation from which all whole and stable relationships spring. When it goes awry or is inconsistent during childhood, the child finds alternative ways to satisfy her hunger for connection and to experience self-worth. Eating disorders are a prime example.

Eating Disorders Develop When There is No Room for Negative Emotions

A child with anorexia, bulimia, or binge-eating disorder replaces the attachment she needs with her family and other significant people in her life with an attachment to food or the use of food. The way she uses food to respond to her emotions communicates the message. The type of eating disorder serves as the metaphorical voice for her experience. It is almost always a way to deny or stem the tide of negative emotional experiences that are not being accepted or tolerated in the family and/or within herself.

I have found that anorexia encompasses the following wishes:

If I do not eat, I will not feel. All the emotions that I need to keep away slip off like Teflon as long as I don't eat. It is only when I put food in my mouth, chew, and swallow, that I begin to experience the deluge of emotions that I long to keep at bay. I'll keep myself small so my emotions are small, too. I feel safe.

The eating disorder tricks the person with anorexia into "feeling fat" instead of feeling overwhelmed by her emotions (emotionally "too fat"). The strategy of starving oneself to keep painful emotions at bay usually works in the initial stages, which is one of the reasons anorexia becomes so powerful. Problems emerge when the feelings return, which they always do. Remember, feelings don't just disappear because we ignore them or pretend they do not exist. In fact, they tend to intensify when we do this. To maintain her distance from her emotions, a person with anorexia then intensifies her ritualized eating or starving to combat the internal swell of emotion. This turns into a vicious and sometimes deadly cycle.

People with bulimia are speaking a similar emotional language as are those with anorexia, but they are communicating in a different way. Control over their life and expression of their feelings are exemplified not through restricting but through purging. Relief for someone with bulimia often comes with the purge rather than in the act of restricting their food intake or when they are eating.

People with bulimia rid themselves of whatever causes the upset through the act of purging. Emotions are kept at bay through discharge and release — through vomiting, abuse of laxatives and/or diuretics, and compulsive exercise. And, paradoxically, the physicality involved in the act of purging is a means to feel what cannot be felt emotionally.

Imagine the act of purging. The mouth is wide open and everything taken in is being vomited out and thrown away. That is what a child who has bulimia is trying to do with her emotional life — make it go away.

From an emotional perspective, someone who binge-eats is using food to stuff down, ease, comfort, disconnect from, contain, or create a buffer against whatever it is that feels uncomfortable or intolerable. In these situations, food can act as a blanket that safeguards the individual from experiencing the feelings that lie beneath.

By replacing an attachment to her parents with an eating disorder, the child may create a more stable world, where she seemingly has complete control, one where her experiences are extremely predictable and reliable. She feels bad, so she doesn't eat (or, at least, doesn't eat anything considered negative), and that makes her feel better. She feels bad, so she vomits (expels the negative feeling), and that makes her feel better. She feels bad, so she stuffs down food (on her emotions), and that makes her feel better.

In this sense, eating disorders are adaptive — they are attempts to replace a missing attachment. But attachments to food do not fulfill the child's need for attachment to a parent or caregiver and other family members.

Though food and bodily obsession become symbolic friends, they offer nothing in terms of human comfort and connection and ultimately they provide little in terms of self-worth, despite the fact that our culture tries to make us believe that thinness and a youthful appearance are the keys to lasting joy and well-being.

What your child needs are deep attachments to her parents — attachments so rich and profound that even the most difficult emotional experiences are met with love and empathy. This is what *true* attachment means; it is a product of mutual respect, trust, understanding, and honesty. It has more to do with how family members treat each other than with how often they see each other, what they do together, what they buy each other, or even how much they know about each other. Recovery for the family is about knowing and accepting each other. To understand what creating this kind of attachment might mean, try the following exercise.

Exercise: What Does Attachment Mean to You

Think of the immediate family members you feel close to. If you don't feel close to any family members, think of other people — more distant relatives or friends outside the family — you feel close to. Then take out your journal and answer these questions. Once you have answered them, consider discussing your answers together as a family.

- What makes you feel close to these people?
- Do you feel like you can tell them about important issues in your life and not feel judged or criticized?
- Are they there for you in times of need?
- Do you feel like they really get who you are?
- Are they honest with you about their emotions and able to express them?
- Are they able to listen to you?
- When you have conflicts with them, are they able to take responsibility for their part in it?
- When they have negative emotions to express, how do they express them?
- Do they like you for who you are, not for who they would like you to be? Do they want you to be someone that you are not?
- Do you feel like they have a hidden agenda or are they up front with you when they ask you to behave in ways that they would prefer?
- Do you ever feel controlled, dominated, or manipulated by them, or that they have unreasonable expectations of you?

As much as you may yearn to share the same kind of attachment with your child as the one you explored in the exercise above, the reality is that it is impaired or damaged. But you can change that. When you do, the eating disorder that plagues your child and your family will have an environment in which to recover. Attachment Theory offers a method for achieving that goal.

Unraveling the Eating Disorder Mystery with Attachment Theory

It is no mystery that people with eating disorders have difficulty experiencing negative emotions. The anxiety and disgust associated with fullness is a metaphor for not being able to tolerate the "full" range of emotions, the "full" experience of being human — an experience that includes sadness, anger, shame, guilt, and many other negative emotions. The need to binge is a way to feel comfort from food when human comfort is not available.

Most psychological theorists agree that anger is a normal and powerful component of the human psyche. How is it, then, that many of my patients with eating disorders never recall having felt anger during their whole lives? Or, conversely, anger is the *only emotion* that they can recall, often covering up more vulnerable feelings like sadness, guilt, fear, and hurt. According to all psychological theories, emotions exist. When emotions are not felt, all psychological theories say that the feelings are being hidden. We often avoid emotions, find justifications for them, or sometimes have a very difficult time even accepting that they exist, despite knowing deep down inside that they do.

Emotions do not go away because a person has decided, either consciously or unconsciously, not to feel them. Eating disorders become a way to channel these difficult emotions. They become a container for the feelings, a place to put them and simultaneously a way to express them. As a result, the eating disorder often begins to feel like it is an entity separate from or a buffer against the internal experience of the person who has it.

Disconnecting the eating disorder from the person's internal experiences often allows her to rationalize it and believe the eating disorder is solely about wanting to be thin or, with bingeing, that it is a way to feel comfortable when there are negative emotions. But the symptoms of an eating disorder represent the individual's states of being, thinking, feeling, and relating — they are metaphors. They are a way for the person to subconsciously deal with an internal emotional experience about aspects to her life that are troubling or conflicted.

In this way, eating disorders become a double bind. On the one hand, the person makes herself think that "there is nothing wrong," that she simply wants to be thin or feel comforted. On the other hand, the disorder functions as the only way she has to deal with her emotions. This double bind is one of the reasons eating disorders are so difficult to treat.

Yet, attachment theory offers a way forward. By recognizing that eating disorders are partly the outcome of faulty attachments, we can begin to create a safe environment for your child to express her emotions. You can become a person she feels safe attaching to. This will help correct the influences that led to the disorder in the first place.

Of course, your child is going to have to do some work as well. Eventually, she will have to see that her eating disorder was a way for her to deal with her painful emotions. She will need to look for healthier ways to express herself.

It can take a long time for your child to grasp that the eating disorder is a response to psychological conflict and a way to contain the conflict and emotions as well. A person who is anorexic or bulimic feels safer when she defines her world by the all-or-nothing rules provided by the disorder — not eating and being thin means she is good; eating signals loss of control and that's bad. A person who binges needs to learn that other people can be more comforting than food. Your child needs to find that her emotional voice can be expressed in better ways than unhealthy eating behavior.

You can help her with this realization by reattaching to her, by developing a strong bond, by becoming the parent you most want to be. The remainder of this book will take you on a journey toward deepening the attachments in your family. If you are successful, you will find a sense of trust, compassion, and empathy with your children as your family moves towards the resolution of the eating disorder.

Relationships of any kind are challenging and none is ever ideal. Attachment theory shows us that caring, connected relationships with others are crucial to our emotional health. Our healthy emotional bonds with our children are the most important gift we can give them. This is the fundamental lesson that attachment theory provides. It is a way forward into a new relationship, one built on trust and responsibility instead of avoidance and shame.

3
Authentic Relationships:
Trust, Empathy, and Responsibility

Stephanie was twelve when she and her father came to see me. Her father was a quiet, conservative man who had been born and raised in India. Stephanie was 5' 1" and rail-thin, weighing only 90 pounds. She wore tight jeans cut low on her hips and a hot pink spandex tank top that accentuated her skeletal frame. Fake rhinestones spelled out "CUTIE" across her chest.

Stephanie's father told me he felt helpless. He hated his daughter's provocative dress, but after insisting she not dress this way in public he discovered that Stephanie carried her preferred clothing with her in her backpack and changed after she left the house. He told me that Stephanie's school called recently because she was wearing a blouse high above her navel and pants low on her hips. He explained that he allowed Stephanie to dress however she wanted for our appointment, because he wanted me to see it for myself.

As he was saying all these things, Stephanie sat expressionless and lowered her head slightly. Her vulnerability was palpable. After expressing his displeasure, he fixed his eyes on me and demanded, "What do you think of my daughter's dress?"

I knew I couldn't answer this question directly. I was being asked to take sides. My first thought was: How can I convey to both of them that the issue is not how Stephanie dresses, but rather what message she's trying to send with her eating behaviors and her choice of clothes? The answer I gave would have a profound impact on whether Stephanie or her father would trust me. Without that trust, this could be their first and last session with me.

I wondered whether Stephanie's father's criticism about her clothing and eating and Stephanie's apparent provoking behavior regarding food and her choice of dress were attempts to convey something more meaningful to each other: the absence of mutual trust. Stephanie's father didn't trust her choice of clothes or her behavior with food (relatively reasonable responses on his part). Stephanie clearly didn't trust that she would be supported emotionally by her father, who made little attempt to understand why his daughter might be doing these things (a relatively reasonable response on her part). And both of them were immediately testing me to determine whether or not I would prove trustworthy.

This is not particularly surprising. Failures in attachment are, at their root, a product of broken or perhaps never-established trust. As we reviewed in the last chapter, the deep bond between parent and child is an inherent need — every child wants to feel connected to her parents. The fact that these attachments may have encountered problems in your family *isn't* because your child doesn't want to be connected to you. It's because your behaviors — verbal, physical, or both — have shown her that bonding with you might be a difficult proposition at best and downright dangerous at worst. Nor can she know that, based on your personal history, a deep level of connection may be difficult for you and that this problem has created the distance or loss between you.

The net result is that your child may not trust you. That doesn't mean you are unfeeling or uncaring. Most likely you have tried to do right by your children. It probably wasn't a set of outrageously abusive behaviors that led your child to question whether or not she could trust you (though, of course, these cases do exist). It's far more likely that through a long series of miscommunications, misplaced emotions, and unnecessarily critical words or actions you have created an environment in which the trust your child would normally have for you has withered and the attachments you both desire have perished.

If failures in attachment find their root in mistrust, then the first step to reestablishing the bonds with your child is to rebuild that trust. But how?

The truth is that there is no magic formula that works each and every time. However, there are a few common factors that form the foundation of trusting relationships. Working on these will help you establish an environment in which trust and attachments can flourish. They are

1. **Refrain from criticism, blame, or judgment.** Though it's easy and sometimes attractive to criticize your child's behavior, blame her for her eating disorder, and judge her for the choices she makes, ultimately it isn't helpful. It creates an environment of shame and in that environment trust can never flourish.

2. **Honestly express empathy, compassion, and understanding.** Empathy and compassion are the cornerstones. You need to learn to understand your child and express that understanding to her. And it has to be authentic. She will see right through disingenuous attempts at compassion.

3. **Take responsibility.** Not only for your role in the development of the eating disorder but also for your verbal and physical actions on an encounter-by-encounter basis.

Each family has its own mix of factors. You need to work on each of these actions consistently as you interact with your child. It's not as though all of you are going to sit down together, you are going to take responsibility for your part in the eating disorder, she will take responsibility for her part, everyone will give a weepy apology, and the problem will magically dissolve. Though an interaction of this nature might be part of your process, the path to healing is just that — a process. It's your ongoing ability to reliably refrain from criticism, express empathy, and take your share of responsibility that will allow your child to begin to trust you. Establishing trust takes time.

Maybe you need to find a whole new way to communicate your feelings and perhaps you need to find a new way to be a parent. Your child will also have to find new ways to communicate and include you in her life in an authentic way. Those tasks aren't easy, but in my view they are worth it. In fact, I believe they are some of the most worthwhile tasks you can undertake.

To help you, in this chapter I will review what it means to refrain from criticism, express empathy, and take responsibility. I will give you examples and exercises that will guide you toward a deeper understanding of these topics and will give you some ideas about how you can implement them in your relationship with your child. The more you are able to do this, the more your child will feel safe to take the leap and trust you with her real self. She isn't going to take this leap minus the safety net; you will become the safety net.

But before I get to that, I want to look at trust for a few more moments. What is it? Why is it so important? And how has mistrust led to your child's eating disorder?

Trust: Showing up for Your Child Emotionally

Defining what trust is and how you know that you can trust someone can be as difficult as describing what love is. To some degree trust is visceral — felt and experienced deep in the fabric of your being. I find it can be helpful for people to have a clear idea of what I mean when I use the word "trust." After all, there are many different kinds of trust; trust isn't a black-and-white issue. There may be some ways your child "trusts" you. For example, you may be extremely consistent in picking her up from school — she "trusts" that you will be there to get her. But you may intuit that isn't what I am talking about. I am more interested in looking at the emotional aspects of the interactions you have with your child.

What I am talking about when I refer to "trust" is your child's ability to rely on you to be present to her emotions — both the good and the bad — without criticizing her, without judging her, without manipulating her, and without running away. It's unrealistic to think that your child should be able to "tell you anything," and certainly inappropriate for her to tell you "everything," but it's extremely reasonable to think that she should be able to bring emotionally loaded material to the table and expect you to act as an adult and help guide her through her dilemma.

I know that sounds like a great idea. You may even believe you already do this. But is that *really* true?

There are a few core components of a trusting relationship you should be aware of. They include:

- **Safety.** The belief that no intended harm will come, e.g., through judgment or criticism.
- **Reliability.** The belief that your responses and reactions will be consistent and similar over time.
- **Honesty.** The belief that you will tell the truth.
- **Empathy.** The ability to experience and deeply understand how someone is feeling, an emotional "holding" of the individual. (There is more on empathy later in this chapter.)

What would it mean for your child to be able to trust you this way on a day-to-day basis? Try the following exercise to learn more.

Exercise: What Would It Mean for Your Child to Trust You?

Imagine your child came home from school one day and said to you:

My life feels completely out of control. I really want to fit in at school, but I seem to be having a hard time at it. I want boys to find me attractive so I feel like I should wear sexy clothes and be super-skinny, even though I don't always feel comfortable that way. You're never there for me. You don't listen to what I say, and, when you do, you just criticize or belittle me. That's why I starve myself. It's the only thing I feel like I have control over and the way to remind myself that I don't deserve anything good. Deep down I believe every judgmental thing you say about me, even though it seems like I don't care what you say. My relationship with food is the most stable and gratifying relationship I have.

How would you react? Take out your journal and try two things.

First, write the most natural response that comes to mind. Be completely honest. Don't edit yourself. Don't try to "do it right" because you're working through a self-help book. I want you to have an honest understanding of your behavior. So take a few minutes and write out exactly how you would feel and what you would say if your child walked through the door tomorrow and said that to you. Or you can use your own recent behavior with your child instead of the example above.

Once you have done that, assume a different role. Imagine you are the best, most understanding parent on the face of the planet. Imagine you are the parent you most want to be — the parent you always dreamed of having when you were young. Let go of all the complicating factors in your life and your family's life that may prohibit you from fully adopting that role. Remember, this is only an exercise. It doesn't mean you have to do this in your daily life. Once you have adopted that role, write a response to the statement above from a place of true openness and love.

Which of these responses is more likely to encourage trust in your teenage child? Does this exercise give you any insight into your own behaviors? You can write out responses to these questions as well if you wish.

Many parents find that when they read something like this, they bristle: "I don't have time for this." "Why worry so much about what other people think of you?" "I'm sure the boys *do* find you attractive, you don't need to wear these clothes." "We're never there for you? Are you kidding me? We've sacrificed our whole life for you. And we criticize you because you don't listen and you're starving yourself. What do you expect?"

These are but a few common thoughts that pop into parents' minds when doing this exercise. Don't beat yourself up if you wrote down things like this in your first response. That won't help the situation. Just realize that you may have some work to do in terms of understanding and empathizing with your child. Perhaps your second response gave you an idea about how you might begin to work toward that goal.

If you got stuck or are struggling to find the words, here are some ideas for the second response. What if you said one or all of the following? "Thank you for telling me this and how you feel." "How can I help you not feel criticized?" "By telling me this I think it helps me understand what life is like for you." "I think sometimes that I say things in an effort to protect you and keep you from feeling bad, but I guess I should be paying attention to exactly how you feel." "Sometimes I feel angry at you because of the anorexia and this makes me say things intentionally to make you feel ashamed. I know this is not fair."

There's no reason to beat yourself up if you didn't respond this way either. These are only a few examples to help you along the road. Responses like these are what your child is craving when she brings her emotions to you — even if she doesn't open up all at once.

The reality is that it's unlikely the scenario in the exercise will ever happen, at least not for a long time. Many well-adjusted teenagers don't communicate with their parents this way, and the psychological, intellectual, and emotional leaps your child would have to make to fully realize that her eating disorder is connected to emotional issues in her life are so significant that they almost surely won't happen overnight.

The purpose of the exercise is to give you a better understanding of what it means to be there for your child emotionally even when she is bringing difficult material to the table. While this interaction has probably never occurred in your real life, how many times has your child come to you with thoughts or feelings that you shut down? Inadvertently or on purpose, shutting your child down is going to damage her trust.

Most people with eating disorders deeply mistrust others. Often they have good reason for that. The people closest to them have proven to be unreliable, inconsistent in their messages, too involved in their own lives, or unsafe in some emotional way, and the person with an eating disorder has made up her mind that the only entity she can depend on is her eating disorder — she does not trust herself either.

For years your verbal and physical behavior has sent your child the message that you aren't willing to open up to her and that you aren't going to tolerate certain kinds of information. Your attachment has been tenuous or has broken down because of this and the eating disorder your family is facing is the result.

Now you have an even bigger challenge to face. The emotional material you are coping with today is *vastly* more complicated. Are you willing to sit and talk with your child about how much she feels she needs her eating disorder, even though you know it to be unhealthy? Are you willing to listen to and try to understand her perspective when she *demands* that the disorder is based on a healthy desire to be thin, even though you know this isn't the case? Are you open to listening to criticism without defensiveness about your parenting, about family problems, and about how these things have impacted your child?

People with eating disorders often feel that others are secretly jealous of their bodies and weight. Thus, they view all attempts at helping them as a surreptitious desire on the part of family members or therapists to make them "fat" — are you willing to listen to that kind of accusation without overreacting? What if your child actually resists treatment because she refuses to "get fat" — can you sit with her then, even though you understand that "fat" has become a metaphor for vulnerability and that what she's really afraid of is experiencing difficult emotions like fear, hurt, rejection, shame, or worse. How will you manage when you begin to realize that some part of her difficulty in experiencing her emotions is due to the fact that you were ill equipped or could not provide a model for her to cope with them?

This is some of what it means to be fully present to your child's emotions without judging them. You are going to have to learn to remain open, even in the most difficult emotional situations, if you want to create an environment in which trust can thrive again. You are going to have to accept your child's mistrust — because she may have learned not to trust you — while at the same time never losing sight of the need to recreate trust.

Don't worry. You don't have to do all of this overnight. It will obviously take patience and practice from all parties. And I do have some techniques that will help you. That's what the rest of this chapter is about. The goal right now is simply for you to begin to understand why your child may not fully trust you now and what it's going to take for her to begin trusting you in the future.

To establish an environment of trust, I sometimes start by telling patients: "Helping you to discover your own voice and your own path is what therapy is all about. My job is to help take care of you, by listening, understanding, teaching, and challenging you to make changes. Your job is to learn how to take wonderful care of yourself. It's my job — not yours — to take care of me. I am here for you and together we will create an environment of mutual respect in which trust will grow and deepen. It is in this relationship that you will discover who you are and learn how to trust yourself and others and be trusted by others."

Replace the word "therapy" with "parenting," and you capture the essence of what it means to raise a child. The core of this message is extremely simple: You are safe with me. Safety is the cornerstone for building trust. Can you communicate that message of safety to your child? How would you do it?

To help you think about how you can start creating an environment in which trust can thrive, I want to give you another exercise.

Exercise: What Would It Mean to Trust and Be Trusted

This exercise is designed to give you a deeper insight into what it means to trust someone, and it will help you take that insight and apply it to the current situation in your family. Take out your journal and answer the following questions. Make sure you come together with your family and discuss your answers once you are finished.

Think of a person you trust deeply. Then answer the following:

- What is it about this person that makes them trustworthy?
- Are you as trustworthy as this person is? Why or why not?

Using this information about trust as a platform, let's look more closely at trust issues in families and apply what you have learned so far to help you establish a better environment for trust to flourish in your own household. Answer the following:

- Give examples of how you see that trust has been breached or broken in your family.
- Why does trust between family members help establish and maintain a healthy attachment to one other?
- What changes do you think you need to make in your family to create greater trust?
- Are you ready to hear what someone in your family tells you about why you are not able to be trusted? Are you prepared to make changes based on what they say?

- How has the eating disorder made the relationships in your family less trustworthy? Are you ready to take responsibility for your part in this?
- What would your family look like if members trusted each other? What would need to change to make this happen? What do you need to change in yourself to make this happen?

Now that we have established what I mean by the word "trust," how that concept or feeling operates in your household, and how you can change to offer your child an opportunity to trust you once more, I want to dig a little deeper and review each of the three factors I identified at the beginning of this chapter that form the foundation of trust.

Criticism: Moving Beyond Judgment and Blame

Many who have eating disorders report that they feel overtly or subtly and frequently criticized, judged, disrespected, and/or misunderstood; as though they are not good enough to fulfill familial expectations; and blamed by their families, not only for having an eating disorder but also for reasons that predate and have nothing to do with the eating disorder. Some fear criticism because their parents are overly demanding and critical, so they try to keep their parents happy by pleasing them or seeking to be perfect for them.

Remember, eating disorders are created not by just one issue but by patterns that are repeated over time. If there is a pattern of criticism, blame, and judgment in your family — especially if it is pointed at your children — this can cause significant problems with trust and attachment. Asking your child questions like, "What are you doing *that* for?" or making statements like, "You shouldn't feel that way," can easily be perceived as criticism and judgment, especially when there is no attempt to try to understand your child's behavior, thinking, or feelings.

There is no mystery about the fact that blame and judgment naturally bring up feelings of shame in the person being blamed or judged. Each of us has experienced it in our own lives — at work, in social situations, and, unfortunately, even in the home.

Where there is shame, trust cannot thrive. Do you trust people who judge or blame you? If you have a history of criticizing her, your child is not going to trust you either. The tender emotions she is feeling are already difficult enough to handle. She is not going to risk bringing them to the surface if she fears she may be made to feel ashamed for sharing them. Always keep in mind that people with eating disorders are burying or otherwise evading their feelings through their behavior. They believe painful emotions are too much to bear, so they stuff them. Piling shame on this only serves to make the problem worse.

However, going beyond criticism isn't always easy. For one thing, many parents aren't clear on how they have been blaming and judging their child. For another, pointing the finger at the person with an eating disorder is extremely easy to do. After all, it often seems that the person "chooses" her behaviors and that she could stop if she really wanted to.

So how do you break out of the cycle of blame and judgment? For an example, let's go back to Stephanie whose story opened this chapter.

Stephanie's Story: Choosing Not to Blame

In Stephanie's family two issues emerged during our first meeting which were manifestations of the same family dynamic. Stephanie's refusal to eat and her inappropriate dress had to do with feeling judged, blamed, controlled, and disrespected.

When Stephanie's father asked me what I thought about her attire, I chose not to make a judgment or blame either Stephanie or her dad. Instead I said, "There's a lot of information I need to know about Stephanie, including a detailed understanding and history of her eating disorder and your family. But I have a hunch that your concerns about how she dresses are also tied up with concerns about her eating. What do you think?"

"She doesn't listen about her eating," her father responded, *"and she doesn't listen about how to dress. She's very stubborn and difficult at home."*

Sensing that Stephanie was feeling very vulnerable at that moment, I knew it was necessary for me to make it clear to her father that I empathized with how she may have been feeling instead of engaging in the blame he was placing on her.

"I see that you have strong feelings about how Stephanie has been behaving," I said, *"but can you also understand that she is probably having very strong feelings herself? Having an eating disorder is not a party for anyone."*

"It has been difficult for her mother and me. We don't know what to do." For a moment he softened, at least to the extent that he was not making a critical statement about Stephanie.

"I understand," I said, *"It is very difficult to think and stay calm when there is fear and when we feel helpless."*

After this exchange, Stephanie's father sat in the waiting room while I conducted an evaluation of his daughter. Now I could ask the question that was foremost in my mind.

"So," I said, *"how did you feel when your dad said that you're stubborn and difficult?"*

"I don't know why I'm stubborn and difficult," she replied.

"So, you agree that you are?"

"Yes, I am, but he makes me so mad."

"It's great, Stephanie, that you know how you feel right off the bat. Sometimes it takes someone with an eating issue a very, very long time to know what she is feeling. But you knew right away. Anger is an important and valuable feeling. What about him makes you so mad?"

"He is so conservative. He doesn't let me do anything. My mom and he tell me what to do all the time."

"Do you know what rebellion is?" I asked.

"Yes, it is when someone fights back," Stephanie said.

"That's right. Not eating is a way to fight back and so is dressing in a provocative way. In both these situations, however, it seems that there are consequences. With one you are hurting your body. With the other you have your school calling home to report that you are dressing inappropriately. So perhaps the forms of rebellion you have chosen aren't particularly useful. You are right to want your parents to get out of your life and let you be more who you really are. You have to figure out how to accomplish this in a way that is healthy for you. I can help your parents learn about trusting you more and about when to get involved versus when to let you figure things out on your own. But, you also need to do your part by figuring out what is really healthy for you. It is all confused now. You are reacting without thinking about the consequences and this will understandably send your parents into a state of fear if they believe you are unsafe."

It's fairly clear that I wouldn't have gotten as much detail and truth from Stephanie if I had been critical of the way she dressed when her father asked me about it. It would have looked like I was siding with her father and reinforcing the judgments he placed on his daughter. This would almost surely have shut Stephanie down.

By the same token I couldn't completely side with Stephanie for a couple of reasons. First of all, her behaviors *were* inappropriate and dangerous. Whether or not I agreed with her choice of clothing wasn't the point. It was causing problems at school and that's cause for concern. More importantly, her eating behaviors were clearly destructive physically and emotionally and I couldn't allow her to think I supported that.

Secondly, I didn't want to drive her father away. If I had taken Stephanie's side and judged or blamed her father, he would most likely have started questioning whether or not he could trust me and if my practice was going to be the right environment for his daughter to heal.

I needed to convey that I was hearing and understanding both their concerns and judging neither of them. By doing this I was able to establish that I was reliable and trustworthy in our very first session. You have the same opportunity with your child. As you work through these exercises, you will learn how to make it clear to her that you are going to put away judgment and blame at the very outset of the process.

The first step is to consciously choose not to overreact or to react quickly. Your emotions *will* be triggered by some of what your child shares with you. These emotions will make you want to judge and blame her. Quick reactions, judgments, and blame of others usually come from feelings and fears within us. Often we reach for anger as a response because it feels less vulnerable than feeling afraid or helpless. Family healing is about choosing not to give in to these reactions and to tap into a deeper understanding instead.

As you begin to speak with your child about the problem, you will feel your emotions rise — your child may even try to intentionally trigger you. When this happens, it's time to take a step back, take a deep breath, adopt your most mature posture, and look for ways you can move forward in the conversation without blaming or judging.

For some of you this may mean learning about the source of your own anger. Perhaps you will come to discover that you too could benefit from your own personal therapy. What a gift that would be to give yourself! Whether you choose to engage in therapy or not, I encourage you to work on understanding how your anger has worked to alienate you from your child and other family members. Anger is a natural response for the family members of someone with an eating disorder. It is also a natural response and often state of being for the person with the disorder. It is a powerful emotion and, when experienced and expressed appropriately, can provide greater trust among family members. But, left unanalyzed or unaddressed, it will only serve to poison your interactions with your child.

You know the old saying: "The best defense is a good offense." Well, it isn't true here. You're going to have to learn to address your angry feelings in a different way. This starts by identifying their source. Perhaps your anger protects you from experiencing deeper feelings of hurt, sadness, or rejection. This is a common experience for parents of people with eating disorders. There are other possibilities as well. Whatever the source of your anger or your child's anger, all the members of your family need to work to understand the source of these feelings — especially when they are used in a defensive, provocative, and alienating way.

For each of you, this will mean watching your words very carefully — examining them for hints of blame and judgment *before* you say anything. This is one of the reasons I recommend writing out your responses to the exercises in this book before you discuss them with your family. It will help you avoid getting caught up in the moment and saying things you don't mean to.

If you regularly take a step back, breathe, and watch what you say, in time you will be able to find ways to express yourself without blaming or judging your child. It won't happen overnight, but it will happen. One of the keys to this process is learning to replace your criticism, judgment, and blame with empathy. When you can tune in to how your child feels and understand it for yourself, blame and judgment will evaporate.

Empathy: Changing Judgment into Understanding

Perhaps the most essential component not only of rebuilding trust but also of reestablishing attachments and setting the stage for recovery is your ability to empathize with your child. If you can learn to do this, the opportunity for healing can emerge. Blame and judgment are vanquished by empathy, trust is founded on it, and attachments come naturally with it.

We will be discussing empathy quite a bit throughout this book. However, I want to introduce you to the concept now because it's so important as you move away from blame and judgment and begin to rebuild trust with your child.

Empathy is the ability to deeply understand what someone is going through emotionally to such a degree that you can truly know what it is like to be in her shoes and respect how she is feeling. Empathy is not an effort to experience your child's emotion yourself or for you to take on her emotions for her. It is an interactive experience, shared between two people. Empathy goes beyond "sympathizing" with your child or simply "understanding her pain." These statements or experiences often carry a connotation of pity or make it sound as though you think of yourself as the great omniscient parent who knows and understands all. Neither of these positions will go over well with someone who has an eating disorder. Your child doesn't want your pity, and she is likely tired of hearing you say that "you've been through what she's going through right now." What she wants is to know that you respect her enough to see her individual experiences as valuable and that you can resonate with these experiences emotionally — that they make sense to you even if you haven't gone through them yourself.

Of course, this is extremely difficult to do when you are parenting a child who has an eating disorder. How can you understand what she is going through? On the surface her behaviors don't make any sense. It probably looks to you like she is intentionally mistreating her body. Even if you know better, it's hard to remain aware of the fact that the eating disorder isn't something she wants any more than you want her to have it.

One way to get past this kind of thinking is to always keep in mind this crucial question: "What purpose does the eating disorder serve in my child's life?" Remember, the eating disorder didn't just happen. Your child did not begin starving herself, bingeing, purging, or eating compulsively on a whim. And she's not doing it because she wants to be thin. She's engaging in these behaviors as a response to some deeper emotional pain. Once you can tap into and *empathize* with that pain, you've taken a major step toward restoring trust, rebuilding attachments, and setting the stage for the eating disorder to resolve.

The key is to put yourself in your child's shoes. This means giving up your personal prejudices, fears, and judgments to some degree, and truly seeing the problem through the lens of your child's experience.

As an example of how you might achieve a more empathetic understanding of your child, I want to introduce you to another young woman I treated and how I helped her parents begin to see that what was going on for their daughter was vastly more complicated and painful than they made it out to be.

Johanna's Story:
From Blame to Empathy — The First Steps

Sometimes trust issues are hidden and it takes some digging to expose them. Johanna was twelve when her pediatrician referred her to me for an eating disorder evaluation. She had been recently discharged from the hospital after treatment for complications due to her low weight. The hospitalization was medical, not psychiatric, and was intended to stabilize her and help her restore weight. When she was admitted, Johanna's pulse was very low at 42 beats per minute and she was severely dehydrated. Her parents were devastated and distraught over their daughter's diagnosis of anorexia nervosa and terrified by how quickly she slipped into a medically critical state.

When I first met Johanna, she showed no outward expression of emotion and she appeared to be in her own world. What Johanna didn't say was, instead, conveyed through her bizarre rituals and behavior.

Her parents reported that she once cut her long, wavy hair on one side only and it took them an entire weekend to convince Johanna to cut the other side before she returned to school.

She washed her hands and face at least five times daily and wouldn't leave her bedroom until her stuffed animals and other possessions were lined up "perfectly" on her shelves. Johanna's compulsive behaviors both infuriated and frightened her parents. They would only understand later that the "perfectly" lined up animals were metaphors for Johanna's wish deep down to be perfect for them and herself, even though she outwardly appeared so oppositional. During the course of her treatment it was revealed that her hand and face washing were attempts to wash away all that felt dirty and shameful about herself and her provocative behavior.

While her obsessive rituals and eating disorder could be interpreted as the onset of serious mental illness, I didn't see them that way. Johanna's behaviors weren't arbitrary or out of her control. Rather, I felt they were deliberate and controllable, as if exhibited for a purpose.

It would take some time to test my thinking. Unlike Stephanie, Johanna did not trust me in our early sessions. During the first five months of therapy, she continually tested the appropriate limitations set by her parents. I remained focused on making sure that Johanna was not a danger to herself, but I also modeled the necessary ingredients for healing and recovery.

During one of our family sessions early in treatment, Johanna's mother expressed her exasperation and terror.

"She keeps doing things that are incredibly provocative and she knows that it infuriates us. The other day, she was outside in the dead of winter in shorts and a tee shirt. It was freezing weather. My husband

went out in the neighborhood looking for her and we couldn't find her until way after dark. We were frantic — we thought she had passed out and was lying somewhere in the snow."

I was horrified by the story and reflected back my feelings of deep concern to the parents. I was planting seeds of empathy in them. While the whole family needed to trust me, it was Johanna, most of all, who had to be convinced I was safe.

"How dreadful for Johanna that she would do that to herself," I replied, "and how sad that this hurtful behavior is acceptable to her. I ask you to think about why she might have done this."

"To get us angry," her father replied.

"Yes, that's true," I responded, "but isn't Johanna also telling you through these behaviors how incredibly bad she feels about herself? Can you put yourself in her shoes for a moment and think about how bad she must feel to treat herself this way?"

Though Johanna's parents weren't yet ready to fully comprehend and accept the amount of pain she was in, when I asked this question I could see the dawn of understanding in their eyes — as if, for the first time, they were beginning to see the problem from their daughter's perspective.

It's time for you to make the same step that Johanna's parents took at that moment. I'm not asking you to completely empathize with your child overnight. That isn't going to happen. Building true empathy and the attachments that come with it takes time. However, you can begin to break the ice and see the situation through your child's eyes. Here is an exercise that will help you do that.

Exercise: Put Yourself in the Your Child's Shoes

To help you begin seeing the eating disorder through your child's eyes, I want you to try putting on her shoes. Think about your loved one with the disorder. (Close your eyes and sit in a quiet spot, if necessary.) Without judgment or blame, think about what this person goes through every day. To help you do this, you may want to reflect on the case histories you've read in this book so far. Then answer these questions. Discuss them with your family after you have written your responses in your journal.

- What kind of emotions does your loved one deal with on a daily basis?
- How would you feel if you had an eating disorder?
- How would you describe the emotions of a person with an eating disorder? Use as many words as you can to describe them.
- What would it be like if you were consumed by thoughts about food?
- What would it be like if you never felt good or even okay about your body?
- How would you feel if the only good days were the days when the number on the scale was acceptable to you?
- How are you feeling now? Do you feel like you have a different understanding of how your loved one feels? In what ways has your view changed?

Now, can you think about sharing your answers with your child? What effect do you think sharing them with her will have? Can you ask her to imagine what it may be like for *you* to be the parent of a child with an eating disorder?

If you decide to share your answers with your child, remember that your goal is to learn how to experience and express empathy. You may find that she is actually able to experience empathy for you in return. How wonderful would it be if you were able to make that first step together?

Responsibility: Owning Your Mistakes

My hope is that by now you have begun to see that blaming and judging your child is not the best course to take to help her heal. I also hope you are beginning to understand that there are at least two sides to every story and that your child has a perspective all her own on her behaviors, her emotional life, and her relationship with you. If you have started to open up to these truths and you can see through her eyes — even a little bit — then you have taken steps on the road to recovery.

The next step, and the final factor in rebuilding trust that I want to discuss here, is taking responsibility for your actions and owning your mistakes.

If you've come this far in the book, you have already accepted the reality that you may have a role to play in your child's eating disorder. As strange as it may sound, I want to congratulate you! That step is an extremely important one in your family's recovery from this problem.

However, if you want to rebuild trust, you have to do more. You have to take responsibility for your interactions with your child and the mistakes you may make along your mutual road to recovery.

The truth is this path isn't perfect. Even if you follow this program step by step, you will encounter bumps on the road. You *will* make mistakes. Most likely you will fall into old patterns of blame and judgment from time to time, even if you don't mean to. You won't always be able to empathize with your child perfectly or see the world through her eyes each time you talk. No relationship is perfect, and I don't want to give you the impression that I have some "pie in the sky" expectations for what it means to be a parent — especially a parent of someone who has an eating disorder.

The key to creating and maintaining an environment in which trust can flourish is not to try to be perfect. Nor is it to ignore mistakes or bury them when they happen. The key is to consistently take responsibility for your mistakes. If you can admit to your child that you aren't perfect, that you are sometimes wrong, and that you make mistakes as a parent, she is far more likely to trust you than if you ignore your mistakes or pretend they don't exist. She needs to count on you to take ownership of your mistakes so that when you point out her mistakes she can believe and trust in your intent to help her and, as a result, learn to take responsibility for her own mistakes. Often it is not the mistakes we make as parents, or even as friends, but our seeking to repair them that speaks volumes about our character.

Think about who you trust in this world. Are they people who pretend they never make mistakes or act in a self-righteous manner? Or are they the people who are humble and down to earth, those who know they are imperfect and are willing to admit and own those imperfections when they arise? Your child is most likely to trust the same kind of person you do.

Becoming this kind of person has a greater impact than you might think. By taking responsibility for yourself and your mistakes you model a mature and adult form of behavior for your child. You show her that it's all right for her to be imperfect as long as she owns up to her mistakes when she makes them. This is an added benefit for your child, and it is one she will be able use throughout her life.

I believe most people know how to take responsibility for their actions as long as they are honest with themselves, so I am not going to give you an exercise to help you learn what you already know.

Instead, I want to share one final story in this chapter. It's about a time when I challenged the tenuous attachment that was growing from a patient to me — I made a mistake in therapy and had to take responsibility for the problem. No one is perfect. Even people who have extensive training in this area, as I do, make mistakes. My hope is that this story inspires you to have the courage to take responsibility in your relationship with your child.

Johanna's Story:
A Therapist Takes Responsibility for Her Mistake

The truth is that Johanna was not an easy case. Her behaviors were quite extreme and worrisome and Johanna herself was very bright and very mistrustful. She never missed a single verbal or nonverbal gesture on my part. She sucked up all the interactions in the room and carefully evaluated each and every one. At times I would glance over to see her eyebrows crinkle as she processed everything that came her way. She was carefully evaluating me during those first five months, not yet ready to dip her toe into the pool of trust.

During most of our individual and family sessions, Johanna refused to sit. She paced the room the entire time. One might assume she kept moving to burn off calories (a typical eating disorder behavior) but I interpreted this behavior as her inability to tolerate being part of her family — the closeness was too much for her to bear. It was also a sign of her emotional agitation, her inability to be comfortable in her own skin. Last but certainly not least, Johanna was trying to infuriate her parents and me.

It's not easy to conduct family therapy when one person is walking about the room. At times I felt like I was a performer in a three-ring circus — so much activity and so many messages being communicated in both verbal and non-verbal ways were often overwhelming. I found myself drained after some of these sessions. Johanna was testing whether I could be trusted. Could I tolerate her provocative behavior by neither approving it nor criticizing it?

Eventually, I decided to confront her behavior a little, to test the waters by asking about it after the fact, rather than confront her when she was actively walking around my office. It was not that I had a particular feeling that the timing was right, it was more like we had reached a plateau and I needed to try something different.

During one session alone with Johanna, I decided to take the plunge.

"Johanna, can you control how frequently you wash your hands and face? And is it that you cannot sit down or will not sit down during our sessions?"

"Yes and will not," she replied, with a smirk on her face.

We both knew her response was an enormous turning point. My relationship with Johanna had been evolving over time. I began telling her, in a playful way, that I had a feeling she knew exactly what she was doing and that she had to feel both good and bad about the power her behaviors gave her. She knew that I knew, and this was a good thing. It relieved her, made her feel safe that someone might understand what she was going through.

Not long after this encounter, Johanna arrived at my office in a particularly angry state. She had regressed to a point I hadn't seen in months. She refused to speak, frequently rolled her eyes, and mimicked how I sat in my chair and held my hands.

Her parents could barely contain their anger and frustration. After a few months of working on eating goals with a nutritionist, Johanna was once again restricting her eating. Her blatant provocation during the session left her parents feeling helpless and infuriated.

At one point I glanced over at Johanna and she appeared indifferent to her parents' diatribe. I felt frustrated and worn down by her behavior. It seemed like we were back at the beginning again. My frustration showed in my expression, as I grimaced slightly.

Almost immediately, I knew I had made a mistake — my reaction fell like a ton of bricks on Johanna. I knew this because there was a moment, less than a second, where I noticed Johanna's face drop and then she quickly resorted to behaving even more provocatively.

The issue at hand between Johanna and me was trust. I felt I had breached it with my facial expression. Johanna knew she had "gotten to me." This had to feel frightening to her. Did she now doubt my trustworthiness? Was I no longer safe for her? Would our work together

continue? I knew there would be emotional fallout if this interaction —
as brief and nonverbal as it was — was left unaddressed.

When I met with Johanna alone later in the week, I started out by
asking how she felt about my reaction in the previous session.

"What reaction?" she responded defensively.

"Johanna," I said, "I know you don't miss a trick. You're tuned into
everything that's said, in both words and behavior. I need to tell you that
I made a mistake when I grimaced at you. I'm sorry."

Silence.

"I think I got caught up in your family's anger at you for not eating.
I also think you were trying to provoke me by mimicking me."

I never said that I felt frustrated by her. I didn't feel I needed to use
that word. We both knew that she had been trying to push my buttons and
I took the bait.

"I know what's underneath all this behavior," I told her. "I also
know that sometimes it's difficult for all of you to tolerate it. It takes time
to understand it. It takes time to understand how to catch it before it
happens. Remember, our work is about helping you uncover the words
and feelings underneath your behavior — especially the behavior that is
provoking your parents and destructive to yourself."

The work we did that day was less about interpreting Johanna's
behavior than about reestablishing and deepening trust between us. My
ability to reflect on my behavior and honestly apologize was crucial to
restoring that trust. I would need to teach Johanna's parents to do the
same thing. They needed to learn how to respect their daughter without
criticism. They needed to learn how to understand Johanna, how to
express empathy to her, and how to be honest with their own feelings.
They needed to learn how to communicate those feelings. Over time,
these were the ingredients that would reestablish and maintain trust in
their family.

These are the same ingredients that will help you heal. It may take time, but it can happen. Taking responsibility for your foibles and mistakes along the way is a crucial piece of the puzzle.

Creating Space for Trust to Flourish

The greatest challenge facing both the person with an eating disorder and the family is to build alternative emotional responses to the eating disorder. Those with eating disorders need their symptoms until they are ready to give them up. Clearly there are some symptoms — such as severe weight loss, not eating for days, or having no will to recover — that require immediate action and intervention and evoke tremendous feelings of anxiety and helplessness. But if the person feels that she is being bombarded by demands, that recovery is more for the therapist and family members than it is for her, or that the recovery process and goals are not manageable or mutually agreed upon, she will usually resist treatment or comply only temporarily.

You have to create space in your home for healing to occur. Don't imagine that the techniques in this chapter or those in the rest of this book are going to heal your family overnight. For trust to flourish again it needs room to breathe. Your child has to feel connected to you, not as though you are pushing her to "achieve" recovery. Refraining from criticism and blame, learning to be empathetic, and taking responsibility for your mistakes will, eventually, help rebuild the trust. But it won't happen if you're dogmatic about it and it won't happen if you insist on perfection or demand that your child engages in a process she isn't ready for.

The key is rebuilding attachment. When you do that, recovery has a greater opportunity to occur naturally. Use the techniques in this chapter to begin restoring trust in your household. But as you do, always remember the essential point — eating disorders become necessary because no alternatives are available. Why would a child develop an eating disorder if her life felt manageable? Remember, eating disorders are adaptations to a life that feels overwhelming and chaotic. In an insidious way, having an eating disorder makes sense.

The best way you can help your child make her life manageable is to be present and empathetic, to talk with her without blame or judgment, and to take responsibility for your actions. Then take a step back and give her some room to grow. As she sees your continued efforts, she will begin to move toward trusting you and you will move toward trusting her.

4
Focus on Family:
Understanding Which Patterns
in Your Family Contributed to the Eating
Disorder

Casey was sixteen when she first came to therapy. She had a robust appetite throughout childhood, but over the previous year had begun restricting her eating and lost forty pounds. She continued to menstruate, but reported that her periods were lighter and lasted fewer days. Although her weight was not quite fifteen percent below normal body weight — a significant benchmark for a diagnosis of anorexia nervosa — she was quickly heading in that direction.

Casey grew up in the affluent suburb of a major city, the younger of two daughters. Her obsession with weight and thinness began when she was ten years old and in the fifth grade. She recalled feeling fat and that her clothing was too large. Casey's mother was participating in a weight-loss program at the time, and, when Casey complained to her mother that she felt fat, her mother quickly "remedied" the situation by asking Casey to attend her weight-loss meetings so they could lose weight together. And so Casey's first diet began in elementary school.

Her mother later admitted to me that Casey's weight at the time was square in the middle of the normal range for her age and height. However, as soon as these words had been uttered, she quickly qualified the statement by saying, "But Casey did have a bit of a stomach." This seemingly innocuous comment revealed much about the mother-daughter dynamic, particularly from an attachment perspective.

The unfortunate pattern illustrated in this vignette is neither as simple nor as unusual as it seems on the surface. To some of you it may appear obvious that encouraging your ten-year-old daughter to attend weight-loss classes with you is probably not a good idea. Yet a startling 80 percent of fourth-grade girls surveyed said they had already been on diets (Brumberg 2000). This shockingly common trend is a reflection of deeper and more complicated social and family dynamics that form the very core of eating disorders.

One question that begs to be asked is why, if she was a normal weight, Casey's mother perceived her daughter as having "a bit of a stomach"? Powerful social influences and her own struggles with weight and body image played their role, as you will see later in this chapter when I share the rest of Casey's story.

However, the questions that are perhaps more to the point, and the ones we are going to reflect on in this chapter are

- How does a young person get to a point emotionally where harming her body with an eating disorder seems reasonable?
- What are the attachment issues at play that contribute to family dynamics that may lead a child to adopt such destructive behaviors?
- Why don't more parents realize this is happening if, in fact, family dynamics and familial attachment are at the root of the problem?
- How can family dynamics be improved so this problem can be overcome?

I assure you there are no easy, one-size-fits-all answers to these questions. Families are complicated and the patterns that define how any one member of the family relates to the others are created and perpetuated for many reasons. Some patterns are adaptive and healthy. Others fuel problematic relationships and behaviors. In many cases, the lines that differentiate these two ends of the spectrum are neither clear nor easily definable. The truth is that the vast majority of parents feel deeply attached to their kids. Most would argue that they have tended to their child's needs to the best of their ability for years. You likely feel, "What went wrong? How did my family get to this awful place?" The question most helpful though is, "What is needed from all family members now?"

An impression I don't want to leave you with is that there is some ideal way to be a parent. There isn't. None of us is perfect, nor can we give our children perfect childhoods or respond to them perfectly all the time. Every parent has failed his or her children at some point. Ironically, it's essential that these failures in attachment occur periodically so the child can develop a sense of autonomy.

An eating disorder is not the outcome of an occasional family problem. Rather, it is the result of many factors likely including poor interpersonal exchanges and failures in attachment that occur repetitively over a long period of time. The stage is set for an eating disorder to develop when these problems become embedded in familial relations. In some cases the patterns are so embedded they are invisible to family members. This makes it that much more difficult to tease apart and change them. In other cases, the problems are quite visible, but the family chooses to look the other way — the elephant sits in the living room, but everyone pretends it isn't there. Such a response is common in families where eating disorders develop and it is almost always destructive.

It's critical that you look at the problems in your family and identify the patterns that encourage your child's eating disorder. Even if families are not able to examine their problems, it does not preclude recovery for a child. Sometimes, families have a very difficult time with change and need to continue to see the eating disorder solely as their child's problem or that their family relationships have nothing to do with the eating disorder. The person with the eating disorder needs in the end, however, to come to accept the realities of her disorder and what is and is not possible in improving her family. Ultimately, her recovery is not based on everyone in the household changing. Choosing to recover is a statement of her decision to be well and have healthy relationships. Perhaps this means that she must come to terms with her own limitations, which includes accepting a family that remains stagnated and unable or unwilling to change. It is an amazing process, however, when a family can move and grow together — cementing their bonds for the future.

In this chapter I will help you analyze how failures in attachment led to dysfunctional family dynamics that contributed to the development of an eating disorder in your child. I hope you understand that in this book it is impossible to cover every single scenario and analyze all of the possible ways attachment can fail. That said, there are some common patterns that I have seen in my practice. To help you begin thinking about some of the ways attachment may have crumbled in your relationship with your child, I would like to share some of the failures in attachment that I see and provide you some exercises and insight into how failures in attachment may have happened in your family.

Typical Failures in Attachment that Lead to Eating Disorders

The following is a list of typical failures in attachment I have seen in my practice. As you review it, keep in mind that failures in attachment can be both subtle and profound. Eating disorders occur in families that range from single parents who have little time to give their child the emotional attention she deserves to families where both parents are seemingly present and available. Eating disorders also occur in families where eating patterns are "normal." There are many ways attachment can fail. These are some of the most common:

- The child feels or is frequently criticized, shamed, or blamed.
- The child is not valued for who she is, is seen as an extension of the parent's unfulfilled dreams rather than as a unique person, and is expected to live up to a parental or family ideal.
- A parent is "controlling," "over-involved," or "overprotective."
- A parent is regularly overindulgent toward the child and is unable to tolerate the child being upset or angry.
- A parent takes a "quick-fix" approach rather than resolving something over time with thoughts, feelings, and reason.
- A parent is unavailable emotionally for the child because the parent is consumed by her own interests or has untreated depression, substance abuse, or an eating disorder.
- A parent feels jealousy and/or envy toward a child, or is disappointed because the child does not emulate the parent.
- A parent has unresolved conflicts from her own childhood and carries them into her relationship with her own children.
- A child is forced to witness marital conflict, is brought into the conflict by parents, or is somehow used as a surrogate, confidant, arbiter, or ally against the other parent.
- A child becomes the family scapegoat.
- Parents measure emotional health by what activities a child is doing or how well the child does in school — the child's value is measured by what the child *does* rather than who she *is*.
- The family cannot identify, put a name to, or discuss emotions. This often leaves a child feeling detached from her feelings or that feelings do not matter.
- A family that reinforces or encourages the child to be perfect is unaware of the pressure and ultimate insecurity this generates in their child.

- A family accepts only positive emotions and denies or suppresses negative emotions or conflicts; common responses include, "Don't be angry," "There's nothing to be sad about," or "Why are you being so emotional?"
- Parents don't allow their child to appropriately work things out on her own or who encourage their child to seek the parents' input, i.e. the "controlling" parent, so that the child doubts her own experience and opinion and may not be able to make decisions on her own.
- A family fails to talk on a consistent basis about significant events and the emotions surrounding them, such as divorce, death, separations, breakups, moving, and other life changes.

Surely, all parents have experienced one or more of these situations. We all make and will continue to make mistakes. Let me reiterate that making mistakes, taking responsibility, and being open to change are *not* indications that there are problems in attachment to your child. In fact, this often means that healthy attachments exist because taking responsibility and being open to reflection and change are indications of your desire to repair and restore the relationship — to remain attached despite the struggles. Problems with attachment, the kind that lead down the path to the development of eating disorders, happen when family members do not relate to each other and fail to show respect and caring in their relationships.

When genuine respect, empathy, and compassion are present overall, a feeling of safety is created and the child develops a reliable perspective about relationships in general. Honesty and guidance on the part of the parents — without control, manipulation, or judgment — allow for the development of trust in the child. When a child is given the right to have her own voice and opinion, self-doubt diminishes. As a result, she learns over time to trust her intuition — that deeply knowing internal voice that guides us throughout life in decision making and assessment of people.

Identifying, discussing, and tolerating emotions among family members, particularly negative ones, creates self-awareness in the developing child — the ability to know, tolerate, and integrate *all* emotions.

When these interactions do not occur regularly in a positive and healthy way, it creates a failure in attachment and eating disorders have an environment in which to flourish. That's what happened with Casey and her family. Long-term, repeated failures in attachment like the ones outlined above set Casey up to develop anorexia. I'd like to share the rest of that story with you now to outline the specific family dynamics that led to Casey's disorder. My hope is that this will give you the insight you need to begin investigating your own family dynamics in the exercises later in the chapter.

Casey's Story: Problematic Patterns

Casey was a normal weight for her age, so why did her mother find it so difficult to accept her daughter's looks? Most children during late elementary and middle school gain weight — nature's way of preparing the body for puberty. For girls, this weight gain, particularly in the torso, is the result of estrogen being stored prior to the start of menstruation. Given that weight gain during this time is a natural and nearly universal phenomenon, it's odd to think that Casey's mother would find it disturbing in any way. Yet this response is far from uncommon.

Casey's mom later told me that she wanted her daughter to "fit in." She noted that her older daughter, Miriam, was slimmer when she was Casey's age — more like her father, who was tall and thin. Casey, she remarked, was built like her — shorter and "fat" around the stomach and hips. Later Casey's mother revealed to me that she had struggled with weight her whole life, that she had never felt like she "fit in," and that she didn't want this for her daughter. By inviting Casey to attend her weight loss classes she hoped to give her daughter "a head start" on staying thin.

Sadly, this is a fairly typical response in our culture, and certainly not unique to families with eating disorders. Having been raised in our thinness-obsessed culture, Casey's mother felt it was natural to "support" her daughter this way. She was obsessed with thinness and it simply never occurred to her to challenge her daughter's — or our culture's — thinking about body image. She honestly believed that the best way to support her daughter was to find ways for Casey to lose weight, rather than help her see the normality and beauty in her own size and shape.

When Casey told her mother she felt fat, she was not looking for a "solution" to the "problem" of being fat. She was seeking a response perhaps more in tune with how Casey was feeling — an empathetic one, one that her mother lacked the awareness to give. Casey's weight was normal and it would have been most helpful for Casey to hear just that. It would have been even more helpful if her mother pressed a bit further and asked Casey why she thought she needed to lose weight. Challenging her daughter's distorted thinking would have been a true sign of support, but this did not happen.

Unfortunately, this was only one among many failures in attachment in Casey's family.

In a later session Casey's mother shared another example of how she attempted to ease her daughter's upset by applying a quick-fix solution. Casey once came home from school upset because she didn't get a part in the school play. Her mom tried to console her by saying, "Don't be upset. There will be another play next term." Although well meaning, this response missed the point entirely. When Casey shared her feelings about the missed part, her mother had an opportunity to support her daughter emotionally. Casey was appropriately upset. An attentive ear, a thoughtful hug, or a comment like, "I know it is difficult to not get what we really want sometimes. I know how disappointed you are." would have gone much farther than an intellectualized response about future plays.

On another occasion, Casey had a huge disagreement with one of her best friends and didn't want to invite this friend to her birthday party. Casey's mother insisted that the friend be invited because not doing so wouldn't be "right." Casey sent the invitation and the girlfriend never responded. This may or may not have been the "right" way to act, but the real issue here was that there was an entire piece missing from their exchange. Her mother never asked Casey how she felt about the friend, what caused the disagreement, how Casey felt about sending the invitation, or how she felt about the girl not responding? Casey's mother simply swept past these complicated emotions. She ignored the communication necessary between mother and daughter for attachment to grow.

Casey told me that this was how her mother typically responded to her feelings — she either minimized them or tried to "fix" them. What Casey's mother didn't realize is that she was developing a pattern that ultimately robbed Casey of the ability to cope with her own feelings and forced her to turn to food instead of family as a container for her emotions.

Understanding Patterns of Failed Attachment

Through Casey's story we can examine some of the underlying patterns of failed attachment that contribute to eating disorders. Part of what's interesting about this story is how normal many of the interactions between Casey and her mother seem. Precisely when interactions like these become "everyday normal," attachment fails. So let's examine the patterns in Casey's family to see if we can gain some insight into the development of eating disorders.

Fixing Problems Instead of Experiencing Emotions

Some parents seek quick-fix solutions to their child's problems instead of sitting, talking, and working with their child to find resolutions that are meaningful to the child. When this happens, they rob their child and themselves of an opportunity to connect with their emotions and deepen their understanding of life. This pattern is extremely common in families where eating disorders crop up, and the irony is that most of the time these quick-fix solutions don't even work.

Consider Casey and her mother. It was second nature for Casey's mom to come up with solutions that she thought would keep Casey from feeling bad. The incident with the school play is a perfect example. Even her attempt to give her daughter a head start on staying thin was, at least on the surface, meant to save her daughter from the pain she had faced growing up.

Given this approach, one can see why an eating disorder looks like a "perfect" solution to Casey. If mom takes a "fix-it" approach, then why shouldn't she? If being thin is a way to fix a problem, why not use it? One of the problems with the "fix-it" approach is that it unwittingly reinforces the notion that the external matters more than the internal. It teaches children that, as long as the problem is solved, the means by which it was solved and the emotional sacrifices made along the way are irrelevant.

"Don't be upset" is a common mantra in our culture and in our homes. But I say, Why not? What's wrong with feeling upset? What would have been so terrible about allowing Casey to feel bad for losing the part in the school play? Would it hurt to recognize and accept Casey's painful feelings regarding her body?

Most of us have the best intentions in the world when we look for solutions to our children's feelings. We don't want out kids to hurt, so we look for a way out of this whole cycle of painful feelings. But experiencing pain and feeling upset are important parts of being a whole person. When we try to fix their problems, all we really do is minimize our children's emotional lives. If this is done consistently, the results can be catastrophic. Casey, for example, learned to respond to her own feelings in much the same way as her mother was responding to them — to have little tolerance for them and to try to fix them. The method she eventually settled on for fixing her feelings was anorexia.

When Casey came home from the play that day, perhaps her mother could have simply said, "I am glad that you know how you are feeling and I understand why you are upset. I'm so sorry, sweetie." You could do the same thing the next time your child brings home painful feelings. This is empathy. Imagine how it might feel.

Unresolved Body Image Issues

Though she never fully admitted to her own body and eating issues or sought treatment, it was clear to me that Casey's mom had conflicts about her weight and body image. Her perception that her daughter "had a bit of a stomach" despite being a normal weight, her description of herself as "short and fat," and the fact that all of this seemed to impact her perception of her social position — remember, Casey's mom never felt she "fit in" — are strong indicators that she had body image issues of her own.

Like sexual, physical, and emotional abuse, body image problems tend to be perpetuated from generation to generation when left unaddressed and untreated. In treatment we found that Casey's own "feelings of being fat" started with messages she got from her mother about weight and the body. Changing these patterns and the messages that come along with them takes significant time and attention. However, it is essential that you pursue this if your child and your family are going to heal. If you have body image issues or have an eating disorder yourself, I *strongly* encourage you to seek treatment. Learning to challenge your own thinking will provide a stronger foundation for your sense of self-worth, self-esteem, and healthy body image. Since children tend to mirror how we behave rather than what we say, modeling a healthy life is the best way you can help your child heal. It has the power to profoundly influence the direction of your child's disorder and may set the stage for you both to resolve your problems and move on to a brighter future. See the Appendix for a better understanding of why therapy is such an important part of the healing process.

Controlling Children Is Not Raising Children

Though it may not be obvious on the surface, Casey's mother was seeking to influence or control Casey's thinking. It was important for her that Casey think, feel, and behave in certain ways. For example, rather than investigating why her daughter was loath to invite her friend to her party, Casey's mother simply insisted that the girl be invited. She could have worked with her daughter to come up with a reasonable solution to the problem she was facing, but opening up and researching possibilities together was not something she was capable of at the time. Similarly, when Casey came home and shared her pain about not getting the part in the play, her mother implicitly suggested that Casey "shouldn't" feel so bad by dismissing her emotional experience. In this sense, Casey's mother was "controlling" Casey's emotional experience.

This sense of parents being "controlling" is something many people who have eating disorders experience. In many cases, the control that the parents model is reflected back to them in the form of their child's controlled intake of food.

Remember, controlling children and raising children are two very different things. Your job as a parent is, first and foremost, to interact with your children in meaningful ways, to provide guidance through imparting your values and sensibilities, and to develop the deep attachments needed to nourish them emotionally. Control represents a relationship of power, not one of mutual interconnectedness, and thus has the capacity to shut down attachment before it ever has the chance to take hold. You will eventually need to learn how to appropriately relinquish control over your children and trust that what you put in over time will not be forgotten in the long run — even when it feels like your child has moved to a distant planet. They need to learn to be adults who are capable of making their own decisions. While this might seem scary on the surface, especially in light of the eating disorder, it's crucial to give your child the autonomy she needs and deserves. If you don't, you may inadvertently perpetuate the underlying issues that are giving rise to the disorder in the first place. In Chapter 6 I will discuss autonomy, why it is important, how to distinguish between autonomy and rebellion, and how to relinquish control while still setting appropriate limits.

Confusing Your Needs with Your Child's Needs

Casey's mother had a strong need for Casey to "fit in" with her peers. Was this an issue for Casey? Did Casey express a desire to "fit in" herself? Did she feel she didn't "fit in" with her peers? We know that Casey had friends and seemed active socially. So whose issue was this really, Casey's or her mother's?

I think we can all agree that the vast majority of children and adolescents have a strong need to fit in with their peer group. This need is a natural part of the process of socialization during this period of life, and most children at some stage have some concerns about "fitting in." The problem here is that Casey's mother never asked Casey how *she* felt in this regard. She simply assumed Casey was concerned about "fitting in" because that's how she felt growing up.

Sometimes we think our children will have the same experiences that we had as children or that we have to protect our children from the emotional fallout we experienced when we were young. But our children may not have the same feelings we had when faced with similar circumstances. They are individuals and may react much differently than we do or did. As parents, we need to be aware of that possibility and find out from our children what *their* experience is, instead of assuming it is the same as our own.

Even if Casey was concerned about "fitting in," there are certainly better ways to help Casey figure out how to do that than focus on weight and body image. Using physical appearance as a mechanism for fitting in is precarious at best — weight fluctuates daily, children's body size and shape change rapidly, and the message is that fitting in comes from the approval of others rather than interpersonal communication and socialization. By focusing on weight and body image you deny your child permission to be who she is. Are these the messages you want to send your children?

Acting "Right"

The last pattern we will explore in this section is the issue of behaving the "right" way, something that was very important to Casey's mother. When Casey decided to not invite her friend to her party, Casey's mother insisted that the girl be invited because it was the "right" thing to do. Let's dig into what this means.

Acting "right" is a complicated issue for human beings. We struggle daily with socialization issues and there are general rules about acceptable actions in each culture. Indeed, I would argue there are some basic parameters around the "right" way to act in our society. For example, if you are walking around your neighborhood and feel like you need to go to the bathroom, you don't simply stop on your neighbor's lawn and do the deed in the grass. This would be "wrong" (not to mention embarrassing). I'm sure with some thought we could all come up with similar examples. There are "right" ways to act.

But is the issue of inviting a particular friend to a party one of them? Was this really an important social lesson Casey's mother was trying to teach, or was it actually a matter of Casey's mother needing her daughter to protect her image in some way? These are important questions to consider and I recommend you investigate them when you face similar situations.

It is sometimes difficult for a parent to remember that the apple doesn't fall far from the tree, and that, given the chance, children will generally act in accordance with their parents' values. That doesn't mean they will do exactly what you would do. If your child happens to land outside the umbrella of what you feel is "right" from time to time, be assured she will probably struggle with her decision and return to the values that were established in your home. Give your child the chance to trust her own instincts and find out what is "right" for her. If she makes a mistake, she will learn from it and change her behavior next time. If you never give her the chance to learn these lessons on her own, you rob her of the opportunity to become a full human being. If she makes mistakes, try and understand that they are her mistakes to make.

Casey's story looks at some of the family dynamics that contributed to the development of anorexia. Bulimia, binge eating, or compulsive eating may come about in similar situations, but the expression of the conflict is expressed through consumption rather than restriction. People who struggle with bulimia, binge eating, or compulsive eating tend to use food to seek comfort from psychological pain, negative mood, or relational strife rather than controlling these emotions through rigidity and restriction. Perhaps Casey's nature was more oriented toward rigidity and perfectionism and so anorexia was best suited for her as the vehicle of expression and metaphoric voice.

Now that I have outlined some of the common family dynamics that lead to failures in attachment, and we have analyzed how such failures in attachment lead to eating disorders, it's time for you to take a look at your family dynamics and see how they may have contributed to the development of your child's eating disorder.

The Dynamics of Your Family

Using the list of common failures starting on page 69, and considering the examples of family dynamics discussed above, I'd like you to do the following exercise. It will help you discover some of the patterns in your family that may lead to failures in attachment and thus set the stage for your child's eating disorder.

To do this exercise, you will need to be completely open and honest with yourself about the problems in your family. I'd like to request that, for the time being, you adopt a policy of radical honesty within yourself. This won't be easy, but your child's health may depend on it. It's time to do the hard work of accepting and assessing your role in the development of your child's disorder. When you are ready, let's begin.

Exercise: Analyzing Family Dynamics and Your Attachment to Your Child with an Eating Disorder

This exercise should be done in two steps as follows.

Step One: Review Your Failures in Attachment

Go back to the list of common failures in attachment starting on page 69. Then open your journal and take notes on any and all of these that apply to your family. As you do so, respond to each question below for each of the common failures in attachment you list:

- Does this problem apply to your relationship with your child? If so, how?
- Outline three examples of how this problem showed in your recent interactions with your child.
- Does this problem apply to your child's relationship to anyone else in the family? If so, how?
- Outline three examples of how this problem showed up in the other family member's recent interactions with your child.

- What are some better ways you could respond in situations like this? You can use some of the examples of alternative behaviors I outlined above in analyzing Casey's story.
- How would it feel to act this way instead of continuing to behave in the same pattern?
- How do you think changing your behavior might change your relationship with your child?

Step Two: How Strong is Your Attachment to Your Child with an Eating Disorder

By completing Step One, you should develop a sense of some of the patterns in your family that led to failures in attachment. Now I'd like you to look at your current attachment with your child in more detail. Think about your child with an eating disorder, then go back to your journal and answer the questions below. Remember, this is a time to be fully honest with yourself and with your child about your attachment. If you can do that, you are on the road to healing. Once you have answered all of the questions in your journal, come together and discuss them.

- Do you feel close to her?
- Do you feel like she can tell you about important issues in her life and that you won't judge, criticize, or blame her?
- Are you there for her in times of need?
- Do you feel you really get who she is?
- Are you honest with her about your emotions? Are you able to express them?
- Are you able to listen to her?
- When you have conflicts with her, are you able to take responsibility for your part in it?
- When you have negative emotions to express to her, how do you express them?

- Do you like her for who she is, not for who you would like her to be? Do you want her to be someone she's not?
- Do you feel like you have no hidden agenda — that is, that you don't need this person to behave in a certain way to serve your needs? For example, are you free of the need to live vicariously through her to fulfill your own unmet needs?
- Do you ever feel you control, dominate, or manipulate her, or that you have unreasonable expectations for her?

The next exercise is designed for the person with an eating disorder. It goes along with the exercise above for family members. If your child is working through this program with you or you have decided to share exercises from the book with her, now is the time to approach her and ask her to complete the following exercise so you can discuss these issues together. Remember, even asking your child to do this exercise is an opportunity to connect with her and express your concerns about her condition. This exercise could also be used by you to look at problems that have been passed down to you from your family.

Exercise: Analyzing Family Dynamics and Your Attachment to Your Parents

This exercise should be done in two steps as follows.

Step One: Review Failures in Attachment in Your Family

Please read through the list starting on page 69 of common failures in attachment that occur in families where eating disorders develop. Then open your journal and take notes on any and all of these that apply to your family. As you do so, respond to each question below for each of the common failures in attachment you list:

- Does this problem apply to your relationship with your parents? If so, how?

- Outline three examples of how this problem showed up in your recent interactions with your parents.
- Does this problem apply to your relationship to anyone else in the family? If so, how?
- Outline three examples of how this problem showed up in your recent interactions with this other family member.
- What are some better ways you could respond in situations like this?
- How would you most like your parents to respond in situations like this?
- How would it feel for you to act in this new way instead of continuing to behave in the same pattern?
- How do you think changing your behavior might change your relationship with your parents?

Step Two: How Strong Is Your Attachment to Your Family Member

Think about your family members — especially those you don't feel close to. If you don't feel close to your parents, that's okay. You should be as honest as you can be with yourself and your parents about this issue. It's your parents' job to cope with difficult emotions that come up for them if you communicate you don't feel close to them — not your job. By reading this book, they will slowly acquire the skills necessary to do that.

Once you have in mind family members you don't feel particularly close to, answer the following questions for each person. After you have answered them, I encourage you to sit down with your parents and share your responses.

- Do you feel like you can tell this person about important issues in your life and not feel judged or criticized?
- Is he or she there for you in times of need?
- Do you feel like he or she really understands who you are? Why not? Give examples if you can.

- Is he or she honest with you about his or her emotions and able to express them?
- Is he or she able to listen to you? What evidence do you have that he or she doesn't?
- When you have conflicts with this person, does the person take responsibility for his or her part in it?
- When he or she has negative emotions to express, how is this done?
- Does this person like you for who you are, not for who he or she would like you to be?
- Does this person want you to be someone that you are not? How do you know?
- Do you feel like this person has no hidden agenda — that is, that he or she doesn't need you to behave in a certain way to serve his or her needs?
- Do you ever feel controlled, dominated, manipulated by this person, or that he or she has unreasonable expectations of you? If you feel manipulated or controlled, how is this done? What unreasonable expectations are you held to?

Once all of you have completed this exercise, I encourage you to come together and discuss these issues.

What Now? Give Voice to the Truth

At this stage you may be asking, "Well, what now? What is the value of understanding the family dynamics that set the stage for my child to have problems? The eating disorder already exists. What can we do about it now?" Let me see if I can shed some light on these concerns for you.

The work you have done in this chapter is crucial because identifying the patterns in your family that led to problems gives you the chance to change your family dynamics and set the stage for healing to take place.

In fact, it is essential that you do so. If we accept the idea that the eating disorders can flourish in families ripe with attachment issues then familial healing can occur more easily when you reestablish these attachments and create an environment where your child can safely communicate her needs, wants, and feelings.

A major task for people who have eating disorders is to learn how to voice their true feelings within the family. Up to this stage, your child may have felt that there was no room for her to do this. She hasn't withheld her true feelings out of a desire to be deceitful or dishonest, but because her fear of rejection, shame, and disapproval was great. Remember, what children see, hear, observe, imagine, and how they are related to by others influences their actions. Changing how you behave and how you communicate has the power to change your child's behaviors. You have the power to create an environment where your child feels safe opening up to you again, or perhaps for the first time. Making this transition is necessary to fully resolve the disorder.

The value of this approach is found in the safety, strength, and hope the familial bond provides. In order for your child to recover, she must believe that her feelings, thoughts, and behaviors will be tolerated by the family, a concept that likely runs counter to her current beliefs or experiences. Identifying your own negative dynamics and patterns can give you the insight you need to make these changes and re-establish your bond with your child. If you don't do this, if you remain defensive about what went awry, or if you diminish or dismiss the feelings and perceptions of your child, your family will have a difficult time healing. That doesn't mean it's your job to "fix" everything that went wrong — you simply need to learn to understand your child in an authentic way and move forward as she learns to understand and trust you again.

Parents can learn to offer continuity, reliability, support, and a non-judgmental attitude to their recovering child. Ultimately what this comes down to is developing a language of emotions. You and your family *can* learn to speak this language. In the next chapter I will teach you how.

5
Develop a Language of Emotions: Learning to Experience and Express Feelings

By relating the events of her life week after week, fifteen-year-old Kelly taught me how devastating it can be for a child to be denied her true feelings. When she came to see me, she had been "experimenting" not only with anorexia and bulimia, but also with cutting herself with razors. This deadly matrix of dysfunctional behaviors went on for three years before she got any relief.

Kelly's parents divorced when she was seven. The split was generally amicable. Her parents maintained regular contact regarding Kelly's care and were agreeable and respectful with each other. Even so, Kelly was suddenly faced with two homes. I was well aware there could be some unresolved emotional issues from this event that contributed to her present problems.

In time I came to realize that the source of Kelly's problems was not the divorce per se, but rather how it and many other situations in Kelly's family were handled. Kelly had been systematically taught to dismiss her emotions for so long that she seemed to have entirely lost the capacity to feel. The only outlets she had left were starving, bingeing, purging, and cutting.

People with eating disorders "learn" not to trust their internal cues. That voice inside us that knows what we're feeling, how we're doing, and what's right quiets and over time is silenced altogether. As you will learn a little later in this chapter, for Kelly this began like it does for many who have eating disorders as a denial of "negative" emotions such as sadness, fear, and anger. Systematic, long-term dismissal of these feelings taught Kelly she could no longer trust her normal emotional responses. She began to doubt her feelings. Doubt led to more denial, and eventually she could no longer hear her internal voice though it was screaming through the gaping wounds on her stomach and thighs and in her attempts to starve herself.

Though Kelly's life may seem shocking, your child may be going through something similar. Even if Kelly's story is not your experience, I encourage you to learn what Kelly's story may be able to teach you about communicating feelings in your own family. Your child is experiencing powerful emotions that she doesn't have the skills or awareness to express. It may seem that she doesn't feel anything at all, that she's numb. She may not even recognize that she *has* emotions. When asked about her feelings, she may respond defensively, not at all, or give you a leaden look and tell you she doesn't want to talk about it. Rather than reacting to situations at school or in the family, using her own internal cues as a measure, she may instead seem calculating, manipulative, disingenuous — as though she's responding to what others expect of her rather than how she honestly feels.

None of this is because your child is inherently cold or deceitful. It's because she doesn't know how she feels, she doesn't know how to talk about those feelings, or she's so terrified her feelings will overwhelm her that she'd rather take cover in the painful yet predictable shelter of her eating disorder.

Just because your child doesn't seem to feel or express emotion or hides behind the mask of manipulation and deceit, that doesn't mean her feelings have disappeared. Like a volcano kept capped for too long, her feelings are raging to the surface in the form of the eating disorder. Bingeing, purging, and starvation are her voice for feelings for which she has no other outlet.

Perhaps the central point of this book is that you and your child, together, must develop the ability to experience *all* feelings, and learn a language that will allow you to express these feelings to each other in constructive ways. To recover from an eating disorder, your child must learn how to identify and talk about her emotional experiences, and you must be present and respond to her empathetically. This process takes many forms and differs from family to family, but it always involves two core tasks:

1. The ability to identify and express difficult emotions, such as disappointment, anger, and loss.
2. A willingness to engage in overt, not covert, communication. This means having open and honest discussions about feelings, family events, and other important incidents in your lives.

In this chapter I will share Kelly's case history, which shows this process in action, and provide you exercises that will help you develop and use a "language of emotions" in your family. The first step is to understand why this emotional language didn't emerge in your family to begin with and why your teenager has developed this intolerance for her emotional experiences.

Learning Not to Feel

Most of us accept that a child learns to speak in good part by being spoken to. We teach them words by repeatedly identifying objects, people, places, and events in our environment. When your child was a baby, how many times did you say, "Can you say mama? Where's mama?" Likely hundreds. Perhaps you remember instances when your infant was sitting in her highchair banging her empty milk bottle or sippy cup. Realizing she wanted more milk, you probably said something like, "Do you want more milk? Mommy will get you more milk." What you were doing in these instances was giving her language — the words she needed to identify who you were and what she was attempting to express by banging her bottle. If she did not learn these words from you or others, it's conceivable she would still be banging her bottle today when she needed a drink. In some ways, that's precisely what's happening with her eating disorder.

Identifying emotions and attaching appropriate language to them is not really any different or more complex than this. Words are needed to label emotions. When a child learns how to talk about her feelings with her family, problems like eating disorders are usually not an issue. Unfortunately, this doesn't always happen. As we all know, emotions are loaded — and there are many reasons why we avoid discussing emotions openly in the family setting. Some adults are unaware of or uncomfortable with their own emotions. If this is the case for you, it's likely you had a difficult time helping your child identify and express her feelings. Some people are simply unaware that using the same method we use to teach our children other kinds of language works for emotions. It may never have occurred to you when your child was young to ask her how she felt or to help her put words to her feelings.

However, the most common problem I see in families who have difficulty with emotional language is a tendency to shy away from painful, negative feelings. Most of us have no problem feeling happy, peaceful, and joyous. These are not emotional experiences we try block out. But when it comes to anger, sadness, disappointment, frustration, pain, or other experiences like these, the story is very different. These kinds of feelings seem to threaten our very core. We worry that our emotions, if indeed felt, will overwhelm us or someone else. How deep can sadness go and will it ever subside, if we finally let it out? How angry can we really get and what effect will the expression of it have on the people around us? Concerns like these drive us to block out our emotions and protect ourselves from them. We may do this by denying that these feelings exist, "No, I don't have a problem at all. Is something wrong?" or avoiding them even though we know full well they're there, "Look, I don't want to talk about it, okay?" or having opposite reactions to our feelings, "I'm not angry at all. In fact, I'm rather pleased," or believing there is no good being upset or expressing it, "After all, what good will it do?" Human beings are clever. We find all kinds of ways to distance ourselves from our emotions. Sometimes we think others are having the emotions we truly have, or we confuse our feelings by saying that we are angry when we are really sad, or experience guilt when we are truly angry or vice versa. We build walls around emotional experience and we hide behind these barricades so we don't drown in a whirlpool of feelings.

If we fear our own negative emotions, then we are uncomfortable at best (absolutely terrified at worst) when our children feel bad. You may be able to handle your sadness, anger, and frustration, but when your child has these feelings, it probably seems intolerable. So we tell our children, "Don't be sad, honey. Everything will be all right. There's nothing to be sad about. Wipe those tears away." We don't want our children to experience the pain of this world, even though we know they inevitably will. We try to protect them from the anguish of their feelings, but by doing so we perpetuate a lie and send the message that it's better not to feel at all than to fully experience the sometimes-unhappy world in which we live. Our attempt to shelter our children ultimately robs them of the words they need to talk about their internal experience. In the worst cases, we set them up to deny this internal experience entirely, and then, over time, their inner voice is diminished and silenced. The sad irony is that by trying to make our children happy all the time, we compromise their ability to live a full and healthy life.

This is precisely what happened in Kelly's family, and the results were catastrophic.

Kelly's Story:
The Danger of Denied Feelings

When I asked Kelly about the divorce, she told me no one had ever talked to her about it. No one ever asked how she felt about it. Upon learning that her parents were breaking up Kelly cried often, a natural response. Both her parents and well-meaning relatives told her that she didn't need to be sad because her mom wasn't sad. Kelly silently reasoned, "How, then, could I be sad?" As a result, she had begun to hide her feelings. In sessions she expressed the feeling that "sad" was not normal or that she would disappoint her mother if she was sad.

According to Kelly, shutting down was not difficult because her family never discussed feelings, especially negative feelings, even before the divorce. She was extremely comfortable when she felt happy, because that emotion was acceptable, but the negative emotions — sadness and anger — were never mentioned. As a result Kelly became very good at appearing happy, even when she wasn't. Shortly after her parents moved into separate places they praised Kelly for moving so easily between the two homes. The transition was anything but easy for Kelly, but she soldiered on, denying her real feelings even to herself.

Despite the tears, Kelly told me that she never recalled feeling sad or angry about the divorce — or about anything else, for that matter. And yet, in the back of her mind, there remained a nagging sensation that something wasn't right. She interpreted this as meaning that she wasn't right. She recalled a chronic sense of emptiness and despair, but she couldn't put her finger on the source.

Kelly had always been a bright and competent student, but she began to struggle academically about six months after her parents separated. Because she was having difficulty concentrating in the classroom, Kelly's parents had her evaluated for attention deficit disorder and other learning disabilities, but the possibility that the divorce may have impacted her performance in school never seemed to cross their minds.

As the years passed and she entered high school, Kelly turned around this trend of difficulty in school. She took her grades very seriously, and at the outset of her freshman year she was at the top of her class. It occurred to me that her scholastic success was a means to paper over the deep sense of loss and insecurity she experienced after her parents separated, but again this possibility was never considered in the family. For Kelly, school organized her life and made her feel normal. It also distracted her from time to think about and experience other aspects of her life and feelings.

It was during the second semester of her freshman year that Kelly first felt fat and cut herself. In fact, the incidents corresponded to a single event: She received a B+ on an English paper and felt furious at herself for receiving such a "low grade." When she arrived home, she ate a snack of chocolate cake and milk and felt worse. Though Kelly was 5'2", athletically built, and was a healthy, slender 115 pounds, eating the cake made her "feel fat." That's when she first cut herself.

She tore through the house searching for some device to do the deed and found single-edged razor blades in the garage. Deciding that marks on her arms would be too noticeable, she settled on her inner thighs and stomach as the destination for her cutting. As she made the first cut into her thigh, she winced from the sharpness of the pain, but as the blood flowed Kelly felt relief. "It was as if a calm fell over me," she told me. When blood stopped oozing from her leg, she made a similar inch-long cut beneath her navel. The physical pain and stinging were more intense

this time, she told me, and the calm afterward was every bit as relieving
and soothing as when she cut her leg.

Why It's Important to Feel Bad

It's so natural for us to stifle negative emotions that the question you
may ask at this stage — and it's one your child may well wonder about at
some point as well — is "Why on earth would anyone choose to
experience emotions that will likely make them feel bad?" The answer is
simple and twofold.

First, we feel emotions all the time whether we want to or not. If we
accept the idea that bonding and connection are driven by our core needs,
then we cannot live without our emotions. Emotions and emotional
interactions are a natural and vital aspect of our existence, one that can't
be quashed by deflection or denial. Left unexperienced and unexpressed,
emotions simply find other ways to make themselves known. Consider
Kelly's case. Her negative feelings were shut down for so long that the
only outlets she had left were cutting and cyclic bingeing, purging, and
starving. These forms of emotional expression may seem radical to you
and, indeed, the emotional outlets any of us use for feelings that
otherwise have no voice vary greatly. A person may feel anxious or
depressed, get sick, or engage in behavioral responses like drinking,
gambling, shopping, or overworking. A person may develop an eating
disorder. These are all methods we may resort to when the free
expression of emotion is prohibited.

Second, emotions can't hurt you the way some of the behaviors
outlined above can. The choice is between feeling and giving voice to
your emotions with words or stuffing them and letting them bubble to the
surface of their own accord. The first is typically far less painful and
destructive. As difficult and powerful as negative emotions can be, they
will not damage you the way eating disorders, addictions, or other

similar behaviors can. In fact, allowing the feelings to come out is good for you and it is an essential step to recovery. The fear of self-discovery, unearthing old wounds, and engaging with painful feelings is enough to make anyone reluctant about seeking help. Transcending this resistance makes recovery possible. The ability to tolerate your fears and move forward will allow your family to begin the work necessary to heal. This is important to keep in mind when you want to run away or shut down emotionally — the ability to tolerate difficult emotions will help you through the scary parts of recovery.

Like Kelly, your child presently feels so threatened by her emotions that she would rather starve herself so she does not feel them, stuff them down by bingeing, or purge them away as the toilet is flushed. She may be doing this because she has become so disconnected from her emotions that she can no longer identify what she is feeling, or she may be doing it because her eating behavior gives her a sense of control she otherwise doesn't feel she has when it comes to the sometimes messy and fickle world of emotions.

Whatever the case, her difficulty expressing her feelings is something, perhaps, that was modeled in your home. If this is the case, then it would be helpful to start modeling something different if you want to help your child overcome her disorder. You can learn a language of emotions and start using it in your home. A good place to start is by reestablishing a connection to your own feelings. Here is an exercise that will help you do that.

Exercise: The Experience of Feeling

Think of time in your life when you felt overwhelmed by intense emotions. Perhaps you felt despair, hopelessness, shame, fear, loss, or sadness. Remember how that experience felt to you. Then answer these questions.

- Name the emotions you felt during this time. If you have a difficult time with this part, the next two pages have a list of words that may help you.
- Did you feel it only in your mind?
- Did you also feel it in your body? How?
- Did you confide in other people about your feelings? Why or why not?
- Did you feel understood by other people? Did they have a sense of what it was like to be in your shoes?
- Think of all the reactions you got from people. Think of the people who seemed to truly understand what you went through. What did they do or say to make you feel that way? Was it their words? Their expressions? Something else? How did you feel comforted?
- If you didn't feel comforted, what could the people around you have done to help you feel safe and secure even in the midst of your difficult feelings?
- Based on your experience, how would you describe empathy?
- How well do you express empathy toward others? What stands in the way of expressing empathy?
- How well do you express empathy for your child who has an eating disorder?

Feeling Words

Happy

amused	animated	at ease	blissful	bright
brisk	buoyant	cheerful	comfortable	content
delighted	ecstatic	elated	enthusiastic	exhilarated
exuberant	exultant	festive	free and easy	frisky
glad	gleeful	great	high-spirited	hilarious
jaunty	joyful	light-hearted	lively	merry
mirthful	overjoyed	peaceful	playful	pleased
radiant	rapturous	reassured	satisfied	sparkling
spirited	sunny	thankful	tickled	transported

Afraid

alarmed	anxious	apprehensive	chicken	cowardly
diffident	disturbed	doubtful	fainthearted	fearful
fidgety	frightened	hesitant	horrified	hysterical
insecure	irresolute	menaced	mistrustful	nervous
panicked	petrified	quaking	reserved	scared
shaky	shocked	startled	terrified	threatened
timid	trembling	uncomfortable	uneasy	unnerved
unsteady	upset	wary	worried	yellow

Angry

acrimonious	annoyed	bitter	boiling	bugged
crabby	cranky	cross	disgusted	enraged
explosive	fed-up	frustrated	fuming	furious
grouchy	grumpy	hostile	hot	impatient
in a huff	in a stew	incensed	indignant	inflamed
infuriated	irate	irritated	mad	provoked
resentful	smoldering	sore	ticked	up in arms
upset	violent	worked up	wrathful	

Annoyed

aggravated	cranky	cross	disgruntled	displeased
exasperated	frustrated	grouchy	impatient	irked
irritated	miffed	peeved	resentful	sullen

Confused

ambivalent	baffled	bewildered	dazed	disillusioned
doubtful	dubious	flustered	hesitant	indecisive
lost	mystified	perplexed	puzzled	questioning
skeptical	stupefied	suspicious	torn	unbelieving
uncertain	unsure	wavering		

Embarrassed

absurd	ashamed	awkward	chagrined	clumsy
conspicuous	contrite	disgraced	foolish	guilty
humiliated	mortified	regretful	remorseful	repugnant
self-conscious	silly	uncomfortable		

Helpless

alone	dominated	empty	forced	fragile
frustrated	hesitant	inadequate	incapable	inferior
insecure	paralyzed	pathetic	reluctant	tragic
useless	vulnerable	woeful		

Hurt

aching	afflicted	agonized	appalled	crushed
dejected	deprived	distressed	grieved	hapless
heartbroken	in pain	injured	offended	pained
piteous	rejected	tormented	tortured	tragic
victimized	woeful	wronged		

Sad

anguished	awful	blah	blue	cheerless
clouded	crestfallen	crushed	dark	dejected
depressed	desolate	desperate	despondent	diminished
disappointed	disconsolate	discontented	discouraged	disheartened
dismal	dismayed	dissatisfied	down	downcast
downhearted	dreadful	dreary	empty	flat
gloomy	glum	grieved	heartbroken	heavy-hearted
hopeless	hurt	in despair	in the dumps	joyless
lost	lousy	low	melancholy	miserable
moody	moping	mournful	out of sorts	pained
rotten	somber	sorrowful	sorry	spiritless
sulky	sullen	tearful	terrible	unhappy
unloved	weary	woebegone	woeful	

Upset

agitated	alarmed	discombobulated		disconcerted
disturbed	disquieted	perturbed	rattled	restless
troubled	turbulent	uneasy	unnerved	unsettled

Tense

antsy	anxious	distressed	distraught	edgy
fidgety	frazzled	irritable	jittery	nervous
pressured	restless	stressed out		

This following version of the exercise is for the person with an eating disorder.

Exercise: The Experience of Feeling

Think of time in your life when you felt overwhelmed by intense emotions. Perhaps you felt despair, hopelessness, shame, fear, loss, or sadness. Remember how that experience felt to you. Then answer these questions.

- Name the emotions you felt during this time. If you have a difficult time with this part, the list of words on the previous two pages may help you.
- Did you feel it only in your mind?
- Did you also feel it in your body? How?
- Did you confide in other people about your feelings? Why or why not?
- Did you feel understood by other people? Did they have a sense of what it was like to be in your shoes?
- Think of all the reactions you got from people. Think of the people who seemed to truly understand what you went through. What did they do or say to make you feel that way? Was it their words? Their expressions? Something else? How did you feel comforted?
- If you didn't feel comforted, what could the people around you have done to help you feel safe and secure even in the midst of your difficult feelings?
- Based on your experience, how would you describe empathy?
- How well do you express empathy toward others? What stands in the way of expressing empathy?

Expressing Empathy and Sharing Your Feelings

Using a language of emotions in your home is simple, but it isn't easy. Take what you learned about empathy in the exercise above. Consider how you would like to be treated during your own emotional crises. Then treat your child that way. If you do this and share your own feelings with her in a calm and adult manner, you will be on the road to providing the emotional support your child needs for recovery.

I grant you that doing this is not going to be as easy as it sounds. Sharing your feelings and expressing empathy for your child is going to be uncomfortable for you at first. Talking about feelings is likely a new language for you or one that you're very rusty at. It's like learning or practicing any new language. It takes time and repetition before you start to feel comfortable using it.

This is going to be further complicated because it's extremely likely that at first your child is going to resist your attempts to communicate about emotions. Remember, people who have eating disorders are fleeing from emotions. In most cases the last thing they want to do is start talking openly about them. Gentle perseverance is the key here. You need to regularly check in with your child about her feelings; you need to share with her how you are feeling; and you will likely need to work on your own parenting style. That means dropping the need to "fix" your child's feelings, learning to tolerate and be present to her negative emotional experiences and pain, and beginning to accept her and praise her for who she is, not just for what she does. All this leads us to our next exercise.

Exercise: Asking Your Child How She Feels and Appreciating Her for Who She Is

Open your journal and take a few minutes to answer the following questions:

- How often do you ask your child about her feelings?
- How often do you ask yourself about your feelings?
- How well is your child able to identify and express negative feelings or experiences?
- Do you take a "fix-it" approach in handling difficult feelings that you or your child have? What have the effects been?
- How well can you tolerate your child feeling sad or angry, without trying to fix her feelings or distract her from them? Is it difficult to allow your child to be sad, angry, afraid, or lonely?
- How well can you allow your child to feel her feelings, no matter what they are?
- Can you allow yourself to feel strong and negative feelings, no matter what they are?
- Can you tell when your child is being realistic about disappointments in her life, and when she is being unrelenting and unforgiving toward herself?
- Can you ask your child how she feels when she does poorly in school or has another type of disappointment?
- In what ways are you proud of your child? Have you expressed this to her recently? How would it feel if you did?
- Do you tend to praise performance or accomplishments rather than the unique qualities that make your child special? Why?
- What would it be like if you allowed yourself and other family members to feel sad, angry, hurt, or disappointed without doing or saying anything to fix or minimize the feelings? What are your fears about what would happen?
- Can you accept what your child has to say, especially if it is about you?

The first steps to healing begin when you are able to ask your child how she feels, and then remain open and empathetic to her response, no matter what it is. When you drop the fix-it approach, when you stop judging your child based on her accomplishments or your own expectations and needs, when you accept her painful feelings without trying to minimize them, then you open the door to trust and attachment. It won't be easy, but the rewards are deep and magnificent. The remainder of Kelly's story will give you a sense of just how profound simply connecting with your child can be.

Kelly's Story:
The Power of Embracing Difficult Feelings

As Kelly talked about the divorce, she began to express how she felt her world had fallen apart. Whosever house she was at, she missed the other parent terribly. At first, Kelly had no idea her eating behaviors and cutting were connected with the powerful emotions she had buried during the divorce. But over time, as we talked together, the connection became clear. In one session she had a powerful breakthrough...

"Kelly," I said, "I want you to think of the moment you're going to eat something healthy and nourishing, but your mind is telling you that it will make you fat. Can you tell me how that feels?"

"I feel scared," she said.

"How scared? Can you describe it?"

"Like I'm jumping out of a plane."

"It sounds like you're jumping without a parachute," I responded, "that there's nothing to guarantee you a safe landing."

"Yes," she said.

"Can you describe the emotions?" I asked her. "Do you feel them in your mind? In your body? Do you just think about them in your head without any sensation of the emotion?"

"I get this sick feeling in my stomach," she said, "and panic sets in, like I almost start to shake."

"It sounds like you're feeling really afraid and unsafe. How will the food hurt you?"

"I know in my head that it won't," she replied. *"I know that it's good to eat and that my body needs it."*

"Kelly, can you remember when you have had those feelings before?"

Silence.

I continued, *"Do you remember a time in your life when you had similar feelings of fear or not being safe or that something bad would happen?"*

"I felt really afraid when I learned that my parents were getting divorced," she responded flippantly. *"I didn't want my dad to leave. I had a sick feeling in my stomach then, too."*

"Kelly, I know that your eating disorder has always felt separate and apart from the events in your life. They are connected, however. For an eating disorder to occur, a variety of things need to happen. Some of these things have more strength than others. You have had a lot of anxiety and loss in your life — the divorce of your parents and, more importantly, the feelings and fears you had about the divorce. No one ever talked about those feelings or thought they were a big deal."

Kelly listened intently.

"It was a big deal to you," I continued, *"as it is for the vast majority of children, especially when they're young. It's easy for a young child to imagine all kinds of horrible things happening. Most of them never happen, but when you're seven years old, anything seems possible. Young children believe in scary monsters, so you can understand how you must have felt when something real and scary happened in your life."*

This was the first time Kelly saw that her eating disorder and life history were intertwined. But she didn't move toward recovery until she started sharing these emotions with her parents. Since she had little experience talking about her feelings and her family lacked a language for expressing them, there was a lot at stake. She feared being seen as "too sensitive," a term her mother used to describe people who "couldn't cope" or "pull themselves up by their bootstraps." She feared ridicule and being shamed. She feared her parents would see her as weak, a belief she held about herself.

When I met with the family, I explained to her parents that Kelly's disordered eating and cutting were attempts to cope, but also to feel emotions she was cut off from. I said that the goal of therapy was to give voice to the emotions that led to the eating disorder. The divorce was very difficult for Kelly, I explained, and she learned from then on to diminish her own feelings. Eventually she lost sight of them and now she has difficulty even identifying when she's having a feeling.

Her parents listened attentively and were as amicable as one could possibly hope for. However, emotion was absent in the room — Kelly's parents spoke very logically, with little emotion, and their moods seemed flat. While they tried to be supportive and accepting of Kelly, they left me with the feeling that they couldn't tolerate any expression of emotion or difference. Their tone and choice of words felt controlling and empty all at once. While I listened, I wondered how Kelly felt.

I asked the parents, "How do you think Kelly felt when you two got divorced?"

"It all happened so suddenly," her mother said. "We made sure she was taken care of and that she had everything she needed."

"But that's not what I asked," I said. "How do you think Kelly felt?"

"I think she felt okay," her father said. "We made sure that she had access to us whenever she wanted and we vowed never to fight in front of her."

"Okay is not a feeling," I said. "Do you think she was sad?"

"She didn't seem sad," her father said.

I turned to Kelly and asked, "Can you share with your parents how you felt when you learned of their divorce?"

Kelly looked sheepish and said, "I felt really scared and sad. I didn't know what was going to happen. No one said anything to me, except you kept promising me that everything would be okay. Somehow I didn't think it was, because all dad's furniture was being moved out of the house." Kelly looked at her mother. "Then you started having all these decorators come in and redo the house. Everyone who came to the house — grandma, Aunt Nancy, and all of your friends — seemed so upbeat, like nothing ever happened," Kelly continued. "Then, when I went to dad's house, he asked me to buy stuff to decorate my new room. I didn't want to do that. I didn't want another room. I just wanted to have it go back to the way it was. No one told me what was going on and then one day it all changed. You all seemed so happy. Did you two ever love each other?"

"Where is that question coming from, Kelly?" I asked. "Why would you ask it?"

"Well, because it all seemed so easy for the two of them. How could people who lived together for so long just end it so quietly? I thought there must have been something wrong with me. And from that point on it seemed like everything needed to be okay. And so I believed that everything was okay and then I started acting like everything was okay."

"I'm so sorry that happened for you, Kelly," her mother said. "You could have told me."

"No, I couldn't," Kelly said. "Don't you see how impossible that was, when it seemed like everything was okay for everyone else? I thought there was something wrong with me. I started believing that nothing that ever happened to me was a big deal. I felt like I had no feelings about anything in my life."

Looking at Kelly's parents, I asked, "Can you understand what Kelly is saying? Can you see how her feelings went underground, how she learned not to listen to them and trust them? How, later on, it seemed like they disappeared?"

"Yes, I see that," said her father.

"What Kelly saw," I went on, "was the elephant in the living room that no one was willing to acknowledge. Soon Kelly stopped seeing the elephant as well. But her mind remembered. The constant denying and shutting down of her emotions eventually led to the eating disorder and cutting. The emotions had to go somewhere."

The look on her parents' faces made it clear to me that we were making progress. They began to understand the relationship between Kelly's feelings and her behaviors. But this was just the beginning of their path toward recovery. In subsequent sessions I worked through many of the same exercises I have shared with you in this chapter and helped Kelly and her family learn to share a language of emotions.

Kelly's father admitted that the process was awkward at first. It was hard for him to ask about his daughter's feelings. Then he said, "But I have to tell you Kelly has made it easy because she tells me it's okay for me to ask. Sometimes she sees me tripping over my words and says, 'Dad, it's okay if you ask me how I am doing or feeling.' It makes me really proud of her when she does that."

It took time for Kelly and her family to integrate a language of feelings into their lives, to rebuild attachments, and to move past the eating disorder. But the process worked, and the proof came several years into Kelly's recovery when her younger sister passed away. Witnessing the impact this devastating event had on Kelly and her family was painful. Their despair was palpable. Kelly had an extremely rough time emotionally. But the family hung together, remain connected, openly grieved for their tremendous loss, and Kelly was able to move through this difficult time without resorting to cutting or disordered eating. In the midst of profound tragedy was the blessing of recovery.

Simply Love

Just as Kelly did, all people need love, comfort, and understanding that are not tied to abuse, shame, criticism, guilt, or rejection. Because it is so difficult for them to understand, this mantra must be repeated time and time again to those with eating disorders. You must learn to say this to your child and you must learn to model it in your daily interactions with her.

Sometimes we all forget how to be empathetic toward one another. This can be especially difficult for parents of teenagers who have eating disorders. Adults typically find it difficult to understand adolescents who, by nature, are simultaneously struggling to reject everything that is childlike and everything that is synonymous with parents. Perhaps you've forgotten what it was like to go through this emotionally loaded period of life, or maybe you were never allowed to feel or express your own emotions when you were young. If you've never had an eating disorder, it may be extremely difficult for you to even begin to understand why someone would engage in such behaviors.

As you develop a language of emotions in your family and you begin to truly listen to what your child is telling you, empathy will bloom because listening to her deeply will enable you to deeply feel for her. You will begin to understand her better, she will begin to rely on you and trust you again, and attachments will reform. This is the road to recovery.

However, as a parent, it is critical that you also maintain your boundaries during this process and that you do not become enmeshed with your child or disavow your own feelings as you are trying to attach to her. You are not learning to breathe the same air. In the next chapter we will discuss why boundaries are important and how you can draw appropriate lines between you and your child. Doing this is just as critical as connecting with her emotionally. When you can achieve connection while maintaining your boundaries, the family dynamic can become rebalanced and the stage will be set for long-term recovery.

6
Create Healthy Boundaries:
Making Space for Your Child to Grow

Karen's mother walked into the kitchen to find Karen pressing down on a chicken breast with a paper towel, carefully squeezing out every bit of "fat" she could extract from the bird. This was a tremendous disappointment as Karen had been in therapy for some time and had recently agreed to add some fat back into her diet. "What are you doing?" her mother screamed, "I thought we were past this. I thought you were eating again." Karen rolled her eyes, snorted, and walked causally out of the room. Later that evening Karen's mother entered the living room where Karen was planted squarely in front of the TV so that no one else could see it. Anger similar to what she felt earlier crept into her throat as she wondered, "Will I be able to manage this situation any better than I did the chicken?"

At some point in the treatment process most parents who are committed to therapy and the recovery process begin to "get it." They understand that broken attachments play a role in the development of their child's eating disorder, they are able to see the ways that attachment has been a problem in their family, and they accept the idea that they need to develop an emotional language to reestablish the bonds the whole family so desperately craves. This is usually the point at which parents come in and say to me, "Okay, we get it. We know we need to work on attachments and emotional language, but we need to be able to manage our child's behavior, too. We are her parents after all, and she *does* have an eating disorder. How do we deal with that in real time? When she comes out of the bathroom after more than an hour, with red and watery eyes, or when she simply won't eat, what do we say then? How do we properly communicate at that moment? How do we explain to her that her behavior is not acceptable?"

This was the conundrum Karen's mother faced. She found herself incredibly upset by her daughter's actions in the kitchen and in front of the television but could clearly see that her gut response — her reaction in the moment — was less than ideal in addressing the difficult situation in an intelligent, meaningful, emotionally connected way. Karen's mother knew that she needed to communicate her feelings to her daughter, and she knew that somehow she needed to manage this difficult behavior. But she did not know how to do that in a way that honored her own needs while not manipulating, shaming, or blaming her daughter.

The question of how to develop appropriate boundaries within the family — especially in a family where eating disorders are present — is a profound one, and it goes right to heart of attachment theory. In the last chapter I explained that creating an emotional language in your family is, possibly, the most important step you can take toward helping your child heal. The fraternal twin of emotional language is proper boundaries. Emotional language is based on safety and trust. Boundaries create that. You are the parent and your child needs you to act like a parent. That means guiding her, explaining where your limitations are, sharing your feelings about her behaviors, and explaining what you expect. The key is learning to do this without control or manipulation. You need to be able to set boundaries in your home and cope with eating disorder behavior while still connecting with your child emotionally.

In this chapter I will provide you strategies that do this. We will look at how Karen's mother finally resolved the situation above and discuss the problem of manipulation and how to overcome it. You will learn how to honor your child's independence while still providing her the dependable support she needs.

But first, I want to explain the relationship between boundary setting and attachments and look at how attachment theory handles the issue of structure and discipline. While it may sound strange at first, what all of this comes back to is the idea that loss and separation are as essential as connection when developing healthy family dynamics.

The Importance and Beauty of Loss and Separation

Up to this point in the book we have been talking primarily about attachment and the importance of developing strong emotional attachments with your child. Now I want to shift toward the concepts of separation and loss and how they are essential features of both attachment theory and raising healthy children. As I have already pointed out, loss and separation are normal and inevitable processes in relationships. To be attached to someone is to set yourself up to experience the pain of loss and separation. In fact, from an attachment-theory perspective the terms are virtually interchangeable[1]: Whether you lose someone you are close to by death or by physical or psychological separation, the emotional response and the impact on attachment are similar. To better understand this, let's consider the concept of separation in the context of the parent-child relationship.

When children are young, they depend on you to sustain their life. Human babies cannot live in the wild without the support and nurturing of mother, father, or guardian. Whoever this person is represents the

---

[1] In this chapter I will use the terms "loss" and "separation" interchangeably.

child's attachment figure. There are essentially two ways this attachment figure can be absent in the child's life: He or she can be either physically absent or symbolically absent. Either way, the child experiences this as loss. Since it is easier to see the immediate emotional effects of physical loss, let's look at that first, and then turn our attention to symbolic loss and how it relates to boundary setting.

Physical loss occurs when the parent is not physically present in the child's life. This can happen through abandonment or death, and it's pretty easy to see the impact such physical absence would have on a child's life. As I mentioned in Chapter 2, early in his career John Bowlby worked with delinquent and maladapted children and found that one of the determinant factors in their problematic behaviors was the physical loss of their parents. He found that children who were abandoned or lost their parents to death were far more likely to become involved in nefarious behavior. While this may sound obvious to us now, it was a revolutionary finding at the time and was one of the discoveries that led to the development of attachment theory.

Over time, attachment theorists have found that physical loss plays an important role in children's lives in more subtle ways as well. For example, there is a period in every infant's life — somewhere between nine and eighteen months — when every time their primary attachment figure(s) leaves the room, the child cries and worries as though that person is never going to return. At this stage of development the child cannot cognitively grasp the concept that momentary separation does not mean permanent loss. You may remember this period in your own child's life. During this developmental period the infant is beginning to understand itself as an independent entity. The parent's temporary absence and the sense of loss that ensues is a critical part of the child's developing self-awareness. Though impossible, let's imagine a scenario where, at this point in the infant's life, the attachment figure never left. It's pretty likely this would lead to problems down the road. Problems would also arise if, on return, the attachment figure simply ignored the child. Most of us intuitively grasp the best path to take in these cases. We leave the room when we need to and when we return, we pick up the crying baby, give it a big hug and kiss, and say, "Oh, sweetie, it's okay. I'm back now."

We can see then that this process of physical loss and reattachment is inevitable and critical in the development of healthy human beings.

Symbolic loss is no less important. This type of loss occurs when the child and the parent become emotionally disconnected from one another. It happens when a person (your child) feels let down, disappointed, criticized, misunderstood, or misrepresented by those she most wishes to trust (you). This type of loss is just as inevitable as physical loss in interpersonal relationships. At some stage every parent misunderstands or misrepresents his or her child. None of us is perfect. There is no way you will ever avoid the type of separation that comes from making mistakes about your child's psychological needs or wants. In fact, these mistakes — these "losses" — are as essential for your child to develop self-awareness as physical loss.

How parents handle separation — whether physical or symbolic — largely determines the child's ability to cope with subsequent loss and difficult emotional material as she ages. Indeed we will all, eventually, experience the ultimate physical loss — death. We will die, our parents will die, our friends will die, and, even though we loathe considering it, our children will die. I say it's better to share this bittersweet reality with our children and provide them with the emotional tools they need to face this moment as best we can rather than deny its existence.

The same can be said for symbolic loss. Your child is going to experience loss in her life and she will experience the emotions that are normally the product of such loss: hurt, sadness, anger, and others. At some point you are going to be the one that causes this loss. You will make her hurt. There's no way around that. The trick here is maintaining balance. When loss becomes pathological in a family, when attachments break, when your child no longer feels like she can trust you at all, when there is an absence of a familial holding environment, when safety, trust, and empathy are weak or non-existent — this is when eating disorders have a climate to develop. These types of long-term losses cause children to become highly sensitized to insults in interpersonal situations. The anger, rage, sadness, and other emotions they experience become too much and the eating disorder becomes a way to deny or avoid them or conversely, to express them.

But you've been doing a lot of work to overcome these problems. By using an emotional language in your home, analyzing your own family dynamics and how they contributed to the eating disorder, letting go of shame and blame, and embracing empathy, you've set the stage for reconnecting with your child. I hope at this point in the book you feel like you are having some success in that process.

To move to the next step in your mutual recovery, you now need to embrace loss in a healthy way. There are methods you can use to share the important lessons loss teaches us without reverting to the pathological disconnection you and your child may have experienced previously. You can speak an emotional language and remain connected to your child while still honoring your own emotions and needs, even in the most difficult situations. The key is to practice setting appropriate boundaries and offer your child the independence she needs to grow. After all, boundaries and independence are forms of loss as well. Let's look at why this is the case and how you can practice better boundary setting in your home.

Boundary Setting and Independence as Forms of Loss

The reason I am focusing on the concept of loss in this chapter is because in many ways setting boundaries is intimately related to it.

Consider what a boundary is in the physical world: a symbol or barrier that divides two things and keeps them apart. In this sense, boundaries imply loss. As with all loss, the outcomes are both positive and negative. When you put up a fence around your yard, you lose the ability to walk freely into the adjacent field. At the same time you provide yourself with privacy and tell your neighbors, "This is mine; that is yours."

As parents, we keep physical boundaries with our children that send them the same message. One example of this is human sexuality and sexual privacy. Though our sexuality exists, how we express it ought to remain a private matter. Often, parents don't understand the full import of setting boundaries in this area.

I believe we would all agree that inappropriate touching of a child or explicit efforts to view a naked child is wrong and indicates serious pathology on the part of the adult. However, many times parents, in their effort to raise children who are comfortable with sexuality, wind up creating more discomfort, anxiety, and embarrassment. Practices such as all family members routinely or "casually" walking around naked, encouraging and continuing parent-child bathing longer than the child is comfortable with (beyond the time when the child becomes fully aware that her own genitalia are a source of pleasure), and walking in on a child in a bedroom or bathroom without the child's permission reflect a lack of appropriate boundaries. Parents need to respect that the development of sexuality really begins at birth and that they need to safeguard that process of development and exploration.

A rule of thumb when it comes to these issues is that more boundaries are better than fewer. Children have very rich, interesting, and sometimes highly charged sexual fantasies about parents and/or other important adults in their lives. To make it safe for your child to experience these fantasies without fear or risk that their fantasy could become reality, parents must refrain from boundary-crossing behaviors.

Symbolic boundaries are the corollary to such physical boundaries. We must turn our attention to symbolic boundaries because this is the type of boundary you currently are dealing with in your relationship with your child. Symbolic or psychological boundaries play a variety of important roles in the family and in the life of the developing child. Many of those roles revolve, in one way or another, around the concepts of loss and separation.

Establishing boundaries allows you to set limits that help define the rules and establish the difference between autonomy and rebellion. So that we are all on the same page, let me explain how I define these terms.

Autonomy is a self-directed act of independence based on thought and reasoning. The outcome of an autonomous act is that you're guided by what is in your best interest. The decision is an outcome of reasoning and judgment. On the other hand, rebellion has no regard for consequences. It is generally based on impulse and unconscious motivations. When someone rebels, she is usually not concerned with the outcome of the act or with self-care or self-protection.

We all know that adolescents are notoriously famous for acts of rebellion. This is normal. They cannot help it to some degree. The area of the brain — the pre-frontal cortex — most responsible for cognitive functions like thought, reasoning, and judgment is not fully developed or engaged. In addition, it is normal for adolescents to psychologically reawaken to the "terrible twos," only this time they are bigger, more hormonally driven, and more psychologically sophisticated. Love interests now are found outside of the family, identity issues emerge, and often the only way they can navigate through this difficult time is to denounce and renounce everything about authority, no matter how benevolent the authority is.

When looked at this way, we can see that on some level the eating disorder is an act of rebellion. Your child is engaging in impulsive behaviors without any regard for the outcome or her well-being. But eating disorders are more than that. Their powerful symptoms represent the clash between two inner voices in your child. One of these voices wishes to use the eating disorder as a statement of her will over others — her independence. The other voice is crying out to be vigilantly cared for and looked after — her dependence. These two voices constantly jockey for a position of dominance within your child, confusing her and potentially keeping her ill for a long time.

Remember that most people with eating disorders view the world in "all or nothing" terms. The notion that a person can have more than one feeling, thought, or outcome at a time is extremely difficult for them to grasp. That she could both seek her independence while remaining dependent on you is not something your child can digest. She simply cannot reconcile these two states of being which coexist in her. Her desires for independence and dependence are at war.

How did this war begin? At this stage in the book you know some of the answers. Repeatedly broken attachments over the long term led to family dynamics that made attachment even more difficult. Over the years this has turned into a downward spiral that contributed to the eating disorder. We have reviewed the processes by which this happens in detail, and I have provided you with strategies to work through these problems.

However, another important part of the puzzle is boundaries. In addition to poor family dynamics, a lack of emotional language, and an environment that emphasizes shame, blame, and guilt, one of the common recurring threads I see in families where eating disorders occur is an inability to set appropriate limits and create solid boundaries for children. This can take many forms, but at its root I believe this happens because some parents fear, or have difficulty with, separation and loss. Some parents may find it difficult to cope with loss because:

- They were never taught how to deal with loss themselves. Their parents may have been deficient in the same skills I have been discussing throughout this book.
- They have a difficult time "sitting with" emotions like anger, sadness, or disappointment.
- They are dissatisfied with their own lives and want to keep their children close to them, creating a situation where the child is the parents' most important source of meaning and purpose.
- The situation actually soothes and sustains some parents, and children remain forever bound and seemingly gratified by the enmeshed relationship. The parent is protected from anxiety and loss, and the proverbial umbilical cord is never severed A classic example of this is mothers and daughters who feel compelled to speak together on the telephone numerous times daily.

Two scenarios arise in response to this problem. The parent may ignore the whole issue of loss, boundaries, and emotional attachment. In some sense the parent is ignoring the child, and letting her "do whatever she wants." However, in the more common scenario that I see, parents fear loss and the difficult emotions that come with it so much that they set too many limits, establish too many boundaries around the child, and thus thwart her independence. When the eating disorder is established, the problem becomes even more complicated. The eating-disorder behaviors are so scary that they induce helplessness and despair in parents who then either forget their rules, in the hopes that if they give in to their child's incessant and often volatile demands she will feel "satisfied," or try to "lay down the law" and "demand" their child correct her behavior — which is a hopeless path in any case.

This is unfortunate, because what any teenager wants, no matter how much she may deny it, is a benevolent guiding force overseeing, setting boundaries and limitations, and establishing and enforcing rules. This makes children feel safe and protected. Once the person with an eating disorder has "gained control of the family" as outlined above, the power she wields leaves her feeling in charge in a way that reinforces how out of control she and the family truly are. Unprotected, and guilt-ridden for knowing what she is putting you through, she suffers silently, and the only outlet she has is to continue or resume her disordered eating.

So when parents say, "Okay, it's time for us to set some boundaries," there is a part of me that says a silent "Hallelujah," because this is *precisely* what is needed in the relationship. It is also an indication to me that the family is ready to deal with the separation issues that will occur as a consequence of this. However, another part of me becomes alarmed because this process is so delicate. The parents and I have to make sure they seek to set boundaries without trying to control their child. We need to make sure they are ready to let go, accept loss, and offer their child the independence she needs. After all, boundaries go two ways. You can establish your limits, but you must honor your child's limits as well. Good boundary setting isn't about control. It is not about punishing your child for her eating disorder or as a way to communicate that you are angry with her for it or other issues. It's not even about ending the eating disorder. It's about teaching your child how to act autonomously not rebelliously. And to act autonomously, your child needs to be independent. That means you have to let go of her, and she has to let you go. That means you both must be ready to experience loss. To see if you are ready for that, let's do an exercise.

Exercise: Why You Resist Loss and Preparing for Loss

This exercise is divided into two parts. In the first part, we will look at the relationship with your child and review some of the reasons you may have resisted the experience of loss and separation, and the difficult emotions that come along with them. In the second part, we will determine whether or not you are ready to take the next steps to begin developing boundaries with your child.

Part I: Reasons You Were Resistant to Separation

There are many reasons parents may resist developing boundaries that allow their child to be independent leading to separation. See if this has been a problem for you by taking out your journal and answering these questions:

- Consider your relationship with your own parents. Were they unnecessarily strict or too relaxed? Were difficult emotions tolerated and addressed in your family or were they shut down? How do you think this has affected your own parenting?
- Do you feel that your own parent(s) were too involved in your life when you were growing up? Conversely, do you feel that they were never or hardly ever around or available?
- Regardless of their involvement with you, were you aware of their rules and familial values?
- Did you feel like they were aware of your needs regarding privacy and boundaries?
- Do you see loss, separation, and difficult emotions as inherently negative and to be avoided, or do you embrace them as part of the human experience? How do you think this influences your life and your parenting?
- Are you satisfied or dissatisfied with your own life? What is satisfactory or unsatisfactory about it?
- Do you worry about letting go of your child? Why? What is this worry like for you?

Part II: Determining Your Readiness for Setting Boundaries and Offering Independence

Now that you have investigated some of the reasons you may resist setting boundaries for your child, let's look at whether or not you are ready to take this step.

- Do you accept the idea that you cannot control your child's behaviors, even her eating behaviors, but can only give her guidance about them? How does that make you feel?
- Are you ready to provide your child the emotional space she needs to become an autonomous individual? Why or why not?
- How much of your past behavior as a parent was directed by the need to soften the experience of loss and the negative emotions it brings up? Why? Do you feel ready to dive into this experience now? If so, why? If not, why not?
- What would it be like for you to communicate authentically with your child about your needs without trying to control her?
- Do you feel like you have the skills and knowledge you need to set boundaries that will guide your child toward independence? If so, write down what it may mean to do that. If not, explain why you don't feel ready.

This following version of the exercise is for the person with an eating disorder.

Exercise: Exploring Boundaries in Your Family

Take out your journal and respond to the following questions as a way to explore boundary issues in your family.

- Do you think your parents are too strict in some ways? If so how? Do you think they are too lenient is some ways? If so, how?
- Do you recognize why setting limits or establishing appropriate boundaries might be a good thing for children? If so, why? If not, why not?
- Do you think that your parent(s) are too involved in your life? Not involved enough?

- Do you know what your family's rules and values are? Do you find yourself regularly challenging them? Do you feel guilty when you don't follow them?
- Do you see loss, separation, and difficult emotions as completely negative and to be avoided, or do you embrace them as part of the human experience? How do you think this influences your relationships with others and with your family?

Your answers to the questions above will give you some sense as to whether you are ready to take the next step in the recovery process. Are you ready to develop boundaries in your relationship with your child that will communicate what you expect while allowing her the independence she needs? If you do not yet feel ready to take this step, I recommend you go back to the preceding chapters and work through that material again, looking specifically for the emotional roadblocks that may be holding you back. When you are ready, the rest of this chapter will explain how to create boundaries and honestly communicate your needs to your child. Let's start by looking at how Karen's mother handled the situation she found herself in at the beginning of this chapter.

Karen's Story:
A Mother Sets Boundaries and a Daughter Responds

The incident with the chicken and the television were only the most recent in a long line of problems Karen's mother faced in trying to help her daughter heal from her eating disorder. Karen's restricted eating had started three years before. That was when Karen first joined the cheerleading squad with her mother's encouragement. Shortly after joining, Karen announced she was "going on a diet to lose some weight so she didn't look fat in her uniform." Empathizing with her daughter's desire for thinness and, perhaps, a bit over-involved in her life, Karen's mother heartily agreed to the idea and even said she would diet with her daughter. Soon they were watching each other like hawks. Karen would snip at her mother if she caught her eating carbs, and mom would snip right back when Karen snuck the occasional chocolate. A subtle competition emerged which Karen was determined to win. Unfortunately, Karen's mother had her own motivations for competing with her daughter. It was many, many months into treatment before Karen's mother was able to say to that her need to compete had to do with her anxiety about getting older and envying her daughter's youth and all the opportunities that lay ahead of her.

After a few weeks went by, Karen's mom reached her goal weight, and went off the diet, although she remained fixated on her weight and her own caloric intake. But, for Karen, there never seemed to be a waist size that was small enough. She continued to restrict her food more radically, and after a few months her cheerleading uniform hung on her like a bag. In three months she had lost 20 percent of her body weight, her menstruation ceased, and she passed out one day at cheerleading practice. It was then that mom decided to get Karen to a doctor and seek some help.

After many months in therapy, and with the help of her doctor and a nutritionist, Karen finally began to turn a corner. Mom admitted she had made more mistakes as a parent than simply agreeing to diet with her daughter, but counted that particular error as a, if not the, triggering event for Karen's eating disorder. The family began to work on using an emotional language and they started to slowly reconnect. It was just about this time that the incident with the chicken and the television occurred.

The moment she walked into my office that day, I could tell Karen's mother had something very important to share. As soon as she sat down, she started to tell the story, admitting that seeing her daughter positioned in front of the TV that way triggered her deeply. She felt extremely angry, but she was also very aware that a battle would ensue if she asked her daughter to move her chair.

Rather than immediately react, Karen's mother took a step back and thought for a moment. She wondered what message Karen might be conveying through her mildly provocative behavior in blocking the TV. That's when it struck her: This was retaliation against the comment about the chicken she had made earlier. You see, Karen's mother had committed to not saying anything about Karen's specific eating behaviors as long as she abided by certain guidelines established with the nutritionist. When she got upset about the chicken and yelled at Karen, she crossed a boundary with her daughter — one that Karen was very sensitive to. Karen's mother admitted she had a weak moment to herself, and again in session with me. This admission opened her to a new way of interacting with her daughter — one that would allow her to honor her own feelings while addressing the situation in a sensitive way that would fit with Karen's needs. Karen's mother recounted what happened next with a sense of pride and satisfaction. Here is what she said:

"I told Karen that I knew she was likely angry because of how I handled the situation with the chicken and that I was sorry. I told her that sometimes it is hard to see her behavior, especially knowing how she agreed to start incorporating some fat in her diet. I explained that I thought this behavior in front of the TV was a reaction to that experience, but it was one that was hostile, self-centered, and in no way verbally addressed what she was really angry about. I said that I was angry as well, but that I was not going to relive that moment with the chicken again. Then I asked her to move over or change her seat so that others could watch TV..." At this point mom beamed and went on, "...and she did!"

She continued, "Shortly after that I walked back in the room, and Karen was sitting on the sofa, bending over, polishing her toenails. I remembered how, in the past, before all of these problems with her eating disorder arose, I would ask if I could give her a kiss, which she always used to allow me to do spontaneously. It had been well over a year since I was able to do that with her, but at that moment something gave me the courage and trust to ask. I did and she allowed me to kiss her."

Mom's eyes welled up with tears and, smile upon my face, I briefly held my eyes closed as a statement of emotional holding of her. Her family was making progress and she knew it.

It was in that moment that I believe Karen's mother understood that there is a typical sequence of events that leads to problematic family relationships and that there are specific steps you can take to resolve these problems in a way that makes sense for everyone involved. Here is the pattern and the process:

1. A breach of attachment occurs — in this case, Karen's mother commented on the chicken despite her agreement not to.
2. The daughter reacts in behavior rather than words — in this case, although she chose to sit in front of the TV, she could just as well have chosen disordered eating.
3. Mother feels angry, and at this point she has a choice — to explode, or to acknowledge her anger yet remain empathetic with her daughter — trying to understand her daughter's emotional response.
4. Assuming the latter happens, mom can then interpret all of this to her daughter, while remaining calm and respectful — in this case, Karen's mother outlined the whole situation using an emotional language.
5. Once the context has been set and the event has been interpreted, appropriate boundaries can be reestablished — here, Karen's mom asked her daughter to move.

6. Because mom established the context and communicated emotionally, her daughter's response was appropriate and respectful instead of raging and attacking.

7. Finally, reattachment needs to take place. In this case, Karen's mother felt the situation was safe and secure enough to ask her daughter if she could kiss her. Due to the course of events, Karen trusted her mother's request and attachment was reestablished.

Obviously, every situation and every family is a bit different, but the course of events here is common across many families and many situations. The critical variable was the mother's ability to step back and look at the situation rationally while still acknowledging her own emotions. If you can do that, you are 90 percent of the way toward building healthy boundaries. Most parents — indeed, most people — know how to communicate what they need well enough. The problem is that we tend to get so wrapped up in our emotions as they occur that our ability to communicate our needs is trampled by our emotional response.

This is why when parents come to my office and wonder, "What do I say to my child when she is bingeing, starving, purging, or engaging in some other provocative or unhealthy behavior?" I usually respond by asking, "What do you *want* to say?" Their answer typically leads us to an understanding of the best response. It is best to know how parents are really feeling about their child's behavior in order to suggest an appropriate way of communicating. Are they angry? Are they worried, scared, or panicked? Are they confused, questioning, or doubting what they've just witnessed? Are they feeling the urge to criticize, blame, or shame the child? Can I then help them communicate their feelings in a non-blaming, supportive way so that they can maintain or reestablish an attachment while honoring their own emotions? That's what Karen's mother did.

The way you communicate at moments like this will either create greater distance between you and your child or help fuel the recovery process. You first need to express your emotions, then, interpret the whole situation for your child, and then set the boundary. This isn't easy. It's made more difficult because you are likely to experience a great range of emotions — love, fear, and anger — all in the same breath. You have a right to your feelings just as your child has a right to hers. That means *all* of your feelings, not just the "right" or "happy" ones. The way you communicate your feelings to your child, when she is in the midst of dysfunctional eating behavior or otherwise stepping over boundaries, is critical. The following exercise will help you identify what you are feeling in moments like these so you can talk about them more effectively with your child. Once you have learned to honor your own feelings, expressing what you need in a given situation will seem natural for you.

Exercise: How to Build Boundaries in the Moment

When you are faced with symptoms of the disorder (such as your child's red face and watery eyes after a long time spent in the bathroom, or the smell of vomit near the toilet) or when you are negotiating other forms of proactive behavior (such as those Karen was engaging in above), take the time to ask yourself these questions and write down responses in your journal *before* you say anything to your child.

- How am I feeling right now?
- Is this feeling appropriate or useful for me to express?
- How might my child be feeling right now?
- What would be most helpful for her to hear?
- How can I say this in a way that honors my feelings and that she can also hear?
- Can I say what I need to say in a way that maintains closeness or connection to my child? How would I do that?

- What is the boundary I need to establish at this moment? What limit am I trying to set?
- How can I impose appropriate consequences in this instance if she does not act responsibly and how can I give her these consequences in a meaningful way?
- How can I encourage my child to seek my support the next time before she acts out her symptoms?

Clearly, these questions are difficult to process in the heat of the moment. That's why I recommend you write down your responses and wait until you have your thoughts together before you speak to your child. Remember, *all* the feelings that come up in moments like these are important. Your task is to express them in a way that honors your feelings and also allows you to remain empathetic toward your child. If you make a mistake, acknowledge it to yourself and your child, and then let it go. Then repeat what you need to say, in a different way. No one should expect to be perfect at this — the freedom to make and acknowledge mistakes is part of the healing and recovery process. Simply do your best to express your emotions honestly, openly, and maturely. Though at first she may not show it, your child will respond very positively to this behavior.

When she is ready, you can share the exercise below with your child. This exercise serves as a sort of counterpart to the one above and will help you discuss the emotional dimensions of the eating disorder in a more sophisticated way.

Exercise: What Purpose Does Your Eating Disorder Serve

The questions below will help you understand that your eating disorder is a mask for deeper emotional issues you are experiencing.

Answering these questions will allow you to identify emotional problems that are contributing to your disorder, and it will help open a discussion regarding attachment issues in your family. The purpose is to help you and your family reorient yourselves toward listening and responding to emotions. Once all of you understand that the eating disorder is just the tip of the iceberg, you will be able to share a language of emotion more easily. This will help you rebuild and maintain your attachments to each other. Take out your journal and answer the following:

- What do you like about having an eating disorder? What don't you like?
- What does it distract you from in your life? What would you pay attention to if the eating disorder were not in the way?
- What does the eating disorder substitute for in your life?
- What purpose does it serve for you in your life?
- What do you really want from yourself and relationships in your life instead of the eating disorder?
- What feelings or thoughts do you think may be present when you are contemplating eating, bingeing, purging, or choosing not to eat? While you are eating, bingeing, purging, or choosing not to eat? After you have eaten, binged, purged, or chosen not to eat?
- Can you see how your eating disorder may be a metaphor for how you feel in your life — may be a way to express through your symptoms what you cannot express through your feelings and words? If so, how?

The Problem of Manipulation

One of the major difficulties that stand in the way of building authentic boundaries in families where eating disorders arise is manipulation. Often parents feel they are being held hostage by their child — that she is making conscious attempts to control them either through the eating disorder or through other psychological means. Many professionals who treat people with eating disorders also describe them as being highly manipulative. While this may be how their child's behavior makes them feel, I typically caution parents (and professionals) to be wary of using the term "manipulative" when describing a person with an eating disorder. Here's why.

Manipulative behavior is often a camouflaged way to get needs met, just as the eating disorder is. Opening up and asking for what they need is often much more emotionally complicated for someone who has an eating disorder than going about getting those needs met in less direct, more "manipulative" ways. Just wanting something can cause guilt or shame. Looking at and learning how to cope with these feelings is simply too difficult, thus the person seeks ways to get her needs met that don't require confronting her emotions. In other cases, the manipulation is an attempt to express hostility that cannot otherwise be expressed. Some wish to control others through manipulation just as they have felt controlled. In all of these cases, what we see is that "manipulation" is not the outcome of some kind of internal personal defect, but rather a complex behavioral response to emotions.

Sometimes the child is quite aware of her manipulative behavior. Other times the behavior is so much a part of her personality that it feels quite natural and is invisible to the child. An excellent example of the latter is people pleasing: the act of making people around you happy so as to mitigate any negative emotional fallout — "If I make you happy, maybe you won't get angry at me." This is common for a person with an eating disorder, and it *is* a form of manipulation.

The apple doesn't fall far from the tree, and parents of people with eating disorders are often just as "guilty" of using manipulation to get what they need out of their children — this manipulative behavior was learned somewhere. This problem typically arises when parents are faced with ambivalence or guilt in getting their own needs met, are fearful about the response their children might have, or when they have their own control issues.

One common form of parental manipulation in families where eating disorders occur is the notion, "If I do X for you, then I expect you to do Y for me." For example, I often hear parents say, "Look at all we've done for you. Why can't you simply do what we ask?" Often, this sets the stage for future guilt (because the child feels bad if she does not give in to what the parent wants), anger, and feeling controlled. The same sort of comment is a form of "guilting" the child into complying with whatever demand the parent makes. This is not an open, honest, authentic way to express a need or request. It's as much of a manipulation as an anorexic child threatening her parents with self-starvation if she can't have the keys to the car.

The problem with labeling your child's behavior as "manipulative" is that the real emotional dynamic is ignored and replaced with a commentary on character that is neither accurate nor useful. What's more, once they label the other person, most people do not take the time to assess their own behavior. By calling your child manipulative, you may be unconsciously denying both your own manipulative behaviors as well as your responsibility in helping create the dynamics in your family that led to this problem in the first place.

To cope with manipulation more effectively in your family, you need to do two things. First, take a good look at your own behavior and the way you treat your child. If you insist that she capitulate on every issue or become the child you "need her to be," she is most likely going to resist you and problems will arise. It's true that some children more easily conform to the familial norm, but often a child with an eating disorder does not. Remember, respecting your child's autonomy while setting appropriate boundaries is critical to the recovery of your whole family. When setting limits or expressing your needs to your child, start with the question, "Is what I'm asking appropriate?" It may be reasonable to expect that your child maintain a curfew, but to demand that she go to the college of *your* choosing is highly controlling and squashes your child's autonomy. This is manipulation, and it will only keep the cycle of manipulation alive in your household. So, take a careful look at your own behaviors and honestly consider whether or not the apple learned it from the tree.

Second, you will have to confront and properly cope with situations where your child attempts to manipulate you. The key is to avoid the trap of responding to the manipulation with reproach, shame, or counter-manipulation while at the same time finding a way to say that you feel you have been manipulated. This is another limit-setting strategy to employ.

To help you learn how to do this effectively, I want to share the story of Hannah, a young lady who learned she could use her anorexia to control her mother — and how her mother eventually learned to confront these situations in positive and useful ways.

Hannah's Story: An End to Manipulation

Hannah had long known she could play on her mother's fear about her anorexia to get what she wanted. When asked to do simple household chores, Hannah would become enraged and vehemently complain that the chores made her tired and dizzy. She knew quite well this strategy would work to get out of chores because her mother was intimidated by anger and confrontation, and the idea that she was making her daughter "sicker" made her feel extremely guilty. What's more, Hannah's mother knew that if she insisted the chores be done, in retaliation Hannah would refuse to eat dinner. Time and time again, Hannah got off the hook from doing dishes and laundry by using these simple but profoundly effective strategies.

In the meantime, Hannah's mother stewed in her anger and shame. She was outraged that her daughter would manipulate her this way and felt incredibly ashamed that she seemed so incapable of getting her daughter to comply with such simple requests. She knew that she had to address this highly manipulative dynamic so that Hannah could have an opportunity to change, and she was well aware that her current methods of coping with the situation weren't working.

That's when Hannah's mother came to see me. Hannah was being treated by another therapist at our treatment center and her mother felt it was finally time for her to come in and try to sort through her own emotions about Hannah's eating disorder and to look for ways to build a healthy relationship with her daughter again.

I coached Hannah's mother on how to honor her own feelings while maintaining her ground with Hannah, and provided some steps for how to deal with situations where Hannah was attempting to manipulate her.

Here are the steps I shared with Hannah's mother:

1. Accept that you *cannot* control whether or not your child will eat. As long as you think you can, she will use that as leverage to make you do what she wants.

2. When she refuses to comply with your requests, ask yourself how you are feeling about your child and her behavior.

3. Once your feelings are identified, communicate them with your child directly. For example, "Hannah, when you refuse to do the chores, scream at me, or do the chore and then retaliate by not eating, it makes me feel enormously helpless, frightened, and angry. I feel torn between yelling back and giving in. I am also aware that it does not make you feel good to know that you are treating me this way and that you are using this behavior to get out of doing the chores. This is not good for either of us."

4. Ask your child what it is like to hear you express your feelings, and allow her to explain her point of view.

5. Ask your child what it is like to be asked to do family chores (or whatever else she is retaliating against) and why she reacts so strongly and provocatively.

6. Ask your child if *she* has a better way to respond to your request *and* get the chores done.

Initially, the idea of doing this caused Hannah's mother a great deal of anxiety. She feared that if she did not give in to Hannah's demands or refusals that Hannah would escalate her eating disorder symptoms and the problem would get worse instead of better. I encouraged her to try using the techniques above and assured her that it was unlikely Hannah would starve herself more in response.

A few days later, when Hannah's mother asked her to vacuum the living room, Hannah started yelling and complaining. This time Hannah's mother was better equipped to deal with the situation. She waited until Hannah stopped and said, "Hannah, when you act this way I feel angry and afraid and worried for you. I don't like being screamed at, but I've been afraid to say anything because I am so scared you will stop eating again. I feel like you are trying to manipulate me, and I'm sure that can't make you feel good. I need your help getting the chores done, and I can't understand why this is such an issue for you. Would you explain to me your feelings on this issue and why these chores are such a problem?"

As it turned out Hannah felt there was an unfair distribution of labor in the household. Her younger brother, who was now twelve, was rarely asked to do chores and Hannah couldn't understand why she should be asked if he wasn't. This inequity had never occurred to Hannah's mother who had become used to relying on Hannah as the eldest child. Once she realized that Hannah was right, her mother began requesting brother's help as well. This made Hannah feel understood, and soon difficulties with household chores were no longer a problem.

I would like to encourage you to use the same system I shared with Hannah's mother for coping with situations where you feel like you are being manipulated by your child. Get some practice at that now with the following exercise.

Exercise: Coping with Manipulation

Please take out your journal and respond to the following:

- Take a few moments to remember and write down a recent time your child used manipulation as a strategy to get what she wanted. Think about how she acted and how you responded. Write down as many of these details as you can remember.
- When your child did this, how did it make you feel?
- Once you have identified your feelings, imagine communicating them to your child. Write down exactly how you would most like to communicate these feelings.
- What would it be like for you to share your feelings with your child this way? Do you feel it would be more effective than behavior you have previously engaged in? If so, why? If not, why not?
- How do you think your child might respond if you communicated with her in this way?
- Imagine asking your child how she feels and what her point of view on this situation is. Write out how you imagine she might respond.
- Do you think your child may have some alternative methods for achieving the same results, e.g., meeting your requests with less emotional confrontation? What might they be?
- Do you have any ideas about other methods you might use to get your requests met that do not involve manipulation?

This following version of the exercise is for the person with an eating disorder.

Exercise: Coping with Manipulation

Please take out your journal and respond to the following:

- Take a few moments to remember and write down a recent time you used manipulation as a strategy to get what you wanted. Think about how you acted and how you responded. Write down as many of these details as you can remember.
- When you did this, how did it make you feel?
- Once you have identified your feelings, imagine communicating them to your parent(s). Write down exactly how you would most like to communicate these feelings.
- What would it be like for you to share your feelings with your parent(s) this way? Do you feel it would be more effective than behavior you have previously engaged in? If so, why? If not, why not?
- How do you think your parent(s) might respond if you communicated with them this way?
- Imagine asking your parent(s) how they feel and what their point of view on this situation is. Write out how you imagine they might respond.
- Do you think your parent(s) have some alternative methods for achieving the same results (e.g., meeting your needs) with less emotional confrontation? What might they be?
- Do you have any ideas about other methods you might use to get your needs met that do not involve manipulation?

Creating Appropriate Boundaries

Among other things, eating disorders are a metaphor for problems with boundaries. People with eating disorders typically do not know what they want in life, what and who is good for them, how they feel versus how they think they are supposed to feel, or whether the feelings and thoughts they verbalize are, indeed, how they truly feel and think. The eating disorder is a representation of this struggle, and through it your child is asking many boundary-related questions: How much food is enough? What do I really want to eat? Am I hungry? Am I not eating because my family is expecting me to eat? Is food the only way to please myself? How do I fit in my family and my world?

Your job as her parent is to guide her through this struggle and help her establish appropriate boundaries. When this is done successfully, it sets the stage for her to begin understanding and asserting how she feels and what is truly good for her. Drawing boundaries is all about reinforcing autonomy, not squashing it. This can be frightening for parents because of the dangers that come along with autonomy. You may ask, "If I really let go, what will happen?" Will she resort to her previous behaviors? Will her eating disorder escalate? Will she keep making poor life choices? Eventually, you will have to let go of these questions, recognize that you can only guide — not control — her behaviors, and hope for the best.

Once you child starts acting in autonomous — not rebellious — ways, it's a good sign that she is entering recovery. When she asserts herself this way, it's likely you will not always see eye to eye. Remember what you have learned about why your trust in her and her trust in you is critical for her recovery. If she does not tell you everything that is going on in her life, it may be that she is exercising her right to privacy rather than being secretive. The right to privacy and autonomy are boundary issues, not statements of disconnection from the family. In fact, if your child feels able to have her privacy and assert her autonomy, that means she is likely feeling safe and secure in your family. Rather than mourning her "growing up," rejoice in her recovery and recognize that you have a role in it.

7
Maintain Healthy Attachments for Life: Recovery and Beyond

Patricia's struggle with anorexia lasted for about two years from the time I started treating her until she went off to college as a whole, healthy young woman. Her problematic eating behaviors began around the time her parents' arguments escalated and their need for her to play the role of "mediator" intensified. For more than a year she resisted the notion that her eating disorder had anything to do with familial issues or the emotional unavailability of her parents, despite the fact that she had physically restrained her father from leaving on more than one occasion. When she finally made the connection and understood the meaning the role of mediator played for her in her parents' relationship, she was able to confront her parents and give voice to her feelings, She saw the relationship to her eating disorder — a key step on the road to recovery.

The tools you have learned up to this point in the book provide all of the basic strategies you need to rebuild attachments in your family and set the stage for your child's — and your family's — recovery. By eliminating shame and blame, by taking responsibility, by developing empathy, by analyzing your family dynamics, by learning an emotional language, by setting boundaries, and by encouraging your child's autonomy, you *can* create an environment in your home in which your child can voice her emotions and experiences with trust and security.

My deepest hope is that you have taken to heart what you have learned in the preceding chapters, that you have used these techniques, and that you have begun to sense a shift in the emotional environment of your home. If this is the case, then your hard work is paying off. Building or restoring a deep and loving relationship with your child and giving her the support she needs to recover from an eating disorder is its own reward. Watching her work toward recovery and bearing witness to the resolution of her problems is likely one of the most profoundly emotional experiences a parent of a child with an eating disorder can have.

However, you may still be left with questions. What does recovery mean? What does it looks like? Does a person every *fully* recover from an eating disorder? What does recovery for the family mean? And, perhaps most importantly, how can I continue to support my child on her journey toward recovery and maintain the attachments we have developed so the eating disorder doesn't rear its ugly head again?

In this chapter, I will answer these questions. We will look at what recovery means from a clinical perspective, both for the family and for the person with the disorder. I will explain why recovery is different for each person, offer some ideas on what it means to raise children in a culture obsessed with body image, and tell you how you can challenge some of the beliefs you may have inherited from that culture. Along the way, I will share Patricia's story and describe what her recovery looked like, and we will analyze what it means to lose an eating disorder and learn to live in harmony once more.

What is Recovery?

One of the most frequent questions I am asked in my practice is, "How will I know my child has recovered from an eating disorder, and is there such a thing as *full* recovery?" This question is extremely important and there is much embedded in it, so I would like to deconstruct it a bit and consider it in some detail. Let's start with the data.

Without treatment, up to 20 percent of people with serious eating disorders die (Kaminker 1998). This tragedy is made all the more painful given the recovery rate of those who do seek treatment, which I will review in a moment. Eating disorders are one of the most lethal psychological illnesses. Anorexia has the highest incident of premature death of *any* psychiatric illness (Sullivan 1995). This why I recommend *the person with the disorder and family members* seek therapy and the assistance of a physician, nutritionist, and other medical and psychiatric professionals as necessary. Even if you have had excellent success with this book and/or other models of treatment, I would still encourage you to look for a therapist who can guide you through the process of treatment and recovery. While the techniques I offer in this book can make a world of difference for families who face problems with eating disorders, the book alone will not completely resolve your problems. In the Appendix, I explain more about why therapy is so important and give you some tips for locating a good therapist.

Though recovery statistics differ, the good news is that between 60 and 80 percent of people who get treatment for their eating disorders recover. That means their weight remains stable and appropriate for their height, age, body shape and size, and gender. They consume a diet of normal foods, and do not feel compelled to eat only chemically altered sugar-substitutes or low-calorie, low-fat, or non-fat foods. They are able to build and maintain both friendships and romantic relationships. They go on to higher education, professional degrees, and careers. Although I am hesitant to use the term, you might say they live a "normal life."

That said, it's important to realize that recovery looks different for everyone. Recovery is a process, typically building over time. It unfolds in response to psychological awakenings, experienced emotions, communication, relational repairs, and behavioral changes. Sometimes it begins with independent insights or revelations. Sometimes the "aha" moment is triggered by the actions or reactions of a family member. In treating many people with eating disorders over the years, I have found that recovery and the exact circumstances that spurred the recovery seldom are the same.

In some cases, people make what you might call a "complete recovery." Their eating behaviors resolve and they do not have any triggers or trigger foods that tempt them to resume their behavior. However, this happens in a minority of cases. Other scenarios are more likely, and these scenarios do *not* mean recovery was any less successful.

For example, some who recover may cease vomiting, but cannot keep any trigger foods in their house for the rest of their life. Others may cease vomiting but, under certain conditions or during emotionally charged situations, avoid foods that will likely trigger a binge-purge episode. Are these people recovered? I say yes, absolutely!

Recovery is not black and white. It doesn't mean simply shutting down the eating disorder. Recovery means knowing what you need in life to go forward and to maintain your capacity to fully experience life and relationships. The benchmarks for recovery are having a healthy relationship with food, connecting with other people in healthy relationships, knowing your limitations, and honoring your feelings. Believing that there is some "perfect" form of recovery generally does more harm than good.

Eating disorders represent, among many things, a belief that perfectionism is the only acceptable outcome in life. Recovery, then, represents the awareness that perfectionism is merely a protection against feelings of vulnerability — typically and unfortunately referred to by people with eating disorders as "weaknesses." Just as it's essential to learn how to integrate and even celebrate both positive and negative emotional experiences, it is also essential to come to terms with the necessary compromises that make a "recovered life" possible. In time, these compromises will no longer feel like defeats, but rather bring a sense of well-being and joy. In order for your child to abandon perfectionism, she must come to know what it is like to trust herself and discover joy and satisfaction in life outside of her eating disorder, including feeling vulnerable.

The truth is that your child *can* get to this place without your help or your intervention. Your family doesn't have to heal for your child to heal. Many people recover from eating disorders without the assistance of family members. However, having the opportunity for the entire family to examine their role in the eating disorder and to create, repair, or build more meaningful, honest, and trusting relationships with each other is, frankly, priceless. Plus, when family members are able to take responsibility, unnecessary guilt that the person with an eating disorder may have placed on herself, evaporates. Vindication is openly provided by family members — the eating disorder is not just her fault — and the whole family shares responsibility for the eating disorder and, more importantly, for her recovery.

If some or all of your family refuses or fails to learn how to use the language of emotions I have been addressing in this book, walls and emotional detachment will likely continue. For the person with the disorder, learning this language of emotions in therapy is an essential feature of healing. If she learns to use it and you don't, one of you might as well be speaking Turkish while the other speaks Greek — you simply won't be able to understand one another. Even if your child does recover under these circumstances, your family's ability to recover is limited and, in my view, that's a grievous mistake. Since you have made it to this point in the book, I assume you take family healing as seriously as I do, so it is worthwhile for us to take a few moments to understand what family healing means.

Healing allows family members to learn not be afraid of each other. They discover what it means to feel safe in confronting and expressing emotion, solid in their belief that their relationships are safe, and to welcome this kind of honesty. As families learn and begin to integrate this new language of emotions into their lives, the veneer of anger, blame, defensiveness, criticism, shame, and guilt slowly falls away. Family members truly begin to understand and accept what it means to openly love each other. They learn how to relate to each other empathetically and share responsibility for their individual contributions in the development of their loved one's eating disorder — and in all aspects of their family life. In time, after the sorrow passes, forgiveness comes and, ultimately, acceptance dawns — each begins to embrace the others' humanity with all its imperfections and contradictions. This beautiful outcome is possible, I have seen it happen in my practice many times, and it is now open to you.

Despite treatment, about 20 percent of people with eating disorders are able to attain only partial recovery. These people typically continue to focus intensely on food, weight, and body image. They usually have only peripheral friendships and often do not have the capacity for romantic relationships — which require real trust, honesty, and reciprocity. Since their attention and energy are spent on dieting and the quest for the "perfect" body, other more nourishing pursuits such as careers and academic achievement are often left by the wayside.

The remaining 20 percent of those who seek treatment do not improve. Often they float from one therapist or inpatient program to another, sometimes they wind up in hospitals as they suffer from some of the more dangerous consequences of eating disorders: heart ailments, dehydration, salt imbalances, or fainting. Those who do not recover usually spend many or most of their adult years with other chronic physical ailments such as gastrointestinal problems, poor teeth, bone mass loss, and infertility. People who do not recover usually do not progress emotionally or interpersonally. Their eating disorder remains their best friend and the only means of emotional expression they ever have. Food becomes family for life.

But let's put aside these scary possibilities for now and focus on what recovery looks like. To illustrate this process in more detail, I would like to share one final case story with you now.

Patricia's Story: A Recovered Life

When Patricia first came into my office, I could see right away that she was bright, articulate, and extremely intellectually talented. On our first meeting she asked where she could find scientific studies that had been published on the use of psychotherapy and other interventions in the treatment of eating disorders. I supplied her with several journal articles to feed her expressed interest and because I was curious about her almost unquenchable need to figure things out on her own. I wanted to gain some insight into the connection between her intellectual life and her eating disorder.

When she returned for her next session, it was clear she had focused almost exclusively on the journal articles that outlined biological models of eating disorders. She had bypassed entirely those that dealt with emotions — those that seemed less quantitative. When I asked her about this, she told me point-blank that she didn't believe her eating disorder had anything to do with her emotions, that she felt fine and that, despite her parents' and her doctor's insistence on meeting with me, she was frankly skeptical of the value of the kind of therapy I provide.

While valuable on one level, her need to make intellectual sense of the world around her was also quite clearly a defense — a way to shield herself from a direct experience with her emotions. When I explained that I felt this may be a possibility, she acknowledged that the idea made sense and that it may be applicable to her, but for the first fourteen months in treatment the message didn't really sink in. She seemed unwilling to think of her disorder as an emotional one — one that was deeply connected to her relationship to her family. Instead, she preferred to think about her anorexia as something purely physical — something she could easily control and fix.

Rather than continue to "fight" regarding the origin of her difficulties, I decided on a different approach. I "took off my lab coat" and used her extraordinarily adept intellect as a tool in therapy. I explained in great detail the various theories about how eating disorders develop and described how her experience might fit into each model. This not only allowed her to trust in my competency and my intentions, but also provided her the opportunity to decide for herself the models that fit best for her. Although my theoretical bias is evident throughout this book, I had no desire to "control the situation" by convincing her that the emotional, psychodynamic understanding in my approach was the right one for her. My real desire was to guide her toward her own recovery and she needed to come to trust that. I believe that relating to her as an intellectual peer opened the door for that trust to flourish.

As a result, over the course of our meetings, Patricia slowly opened up to me and began sharing details of her family life. She revealed that she often found herself in the middle of her parents' arguments, playing moderator between them — specifically, she advocated on her mother's behalf as a means to keep her father in the home. On two occasions, she physically prevented her father from leaving the house and, despite his insistence that he wanted to leave, he returned for her. She described the anger, frustration, and shame she felt about having parents whom she described as "incapable of taking care of themselves" and how she often experienced guilt when she couldn't find a resolution to her parents' conflicts or work out adequate compromises or other arrangements on their behalf — the child taking care of the parents is the ideal "emotional cocktail" for development of an eating disorder — and her eating disorder arose.

Despite these revelations in therapy, she was slow to accept the idea that her behaviors were connected to her emotions. Only when she shared with me a dream that she had one night, did Patricia have her "aha" moment and wake up to the profound relationship between her emotional life and her anorexia.

In the dream, Patricia was standing over a child that was "covered in food and was a mess." Both of her parents were standing next to her in the dream, but they didn't make a move to console or clean up the child. As in her waking life, Patricia was the one to take charge in her nocturnal reverie: "I cleaned up the little girl, then held her, tucked her in bed, and kissed her cheek," she reported. After Patricia finished describing her dream, I asked how she felt about it. She said, "I think I have been having a lot of feelings for a long time, and I've been denying them. I feel sad for the girl in the dream, and I realize that must mean on some level I feel sorry for myself. The food was all over me."

"Though it was written all over your face, the food was not in you," I said.

By saying this out loud, Patricia began to see how she had been shielding herself from her painful feelings by starving herself. Her anorexia was a metaphor for her parent's lack of empathetic care. She was in part starving herself of the nourishment her body needed, just as they had starved her of the emotional nourishment her psyche needed. She was not receiving the emotional food she required to feel safe and secure, and therefore had begun denying herself the dietary requirements of her body.

For the first time, Patricia was able to connect with the deep despair she carried for taking care of her parent when they should have been taking care of her. She also understood that, unless she could fully reconnect with all her feelings and learn to express them, she would likely stay forever trapped in the nightmare of attempting to control her emotions by controlling her eating. Patricia expressed the terror, sadness, and rejection she felt about her father's attempts to leave the house. However, she also felt confused and ambivalent about the fact that she was the one who could make her father return. This internal conflict was avoided by not eating, and she openly acknowledged that as long she remained sick, her father was unlikely to leave.

It was at this point that Patricia asked her parents to attend family therapy with her. Family therapy allowed her to voice her emotions to her parents in a safe environment and in turn provided her the opportunity to better understand her feelings and her parents. Over the course of the conversations that were held in my office, Patricia's parents finally heard why she had kept silent for so long out of fear of rocking the boat. As she related her emotional experience, Patricia found a very powerful, authentic, sensitive voice. She remained empathetic toward her parents and the problems they faced in their marriage while letting them know how hard she worked to try to keep everything together in their family. Patricia spoke candidly about how guilty she felt about going away to college and leaving her parents at home without her to mediate their arguments. She wept as she shared her fear that when she left, her parent's marriage would finally fall apart and the family would be splintered.

Her parents were remarkably understanding and supportive. They sat with her emotions, complimented her on her maturity, and even said that they felt Patricia understood them more than they understood themselves. While well intentioned, this later statement was something of a mixed blessing, as it represented yet another instance of her parents need for Patricia to take care of them. Nonetheless, by speaking her mind, Patricia finally came to the realization that she did not have the power to change her parents' relationship, and she told them as much. She realized that her only true power — the only real power any of us have — was to shape her life into what she most wanted it to be. By working so hard all those years to keep her parents' marriage intact, she had denied herself this birthright, and in doing so she had buried her emotions and lived in a world that demanded numbness and perfection to succeed and survive. Slowly, Patricia was giving up that world.

In conjunction with therapy, Patricia was meeting with a nutritionist and came to understand what her body needed to stay healthy, just as she had realized what her psyche needed to remain stable. By eating based on these good nutritional standards, over time her menstrual cycle returned and her symptoms began to fade. She stopped starving herself, began to consume 2000 calories a day, the amount appropriate for her, agreed to eat more calories on the days she exercised, and routinely ate three meals a day.

Was her relationship with food "perfect?" No. She still had some difficulties. She admitted that she saw food as medicine she had to take to stay healthy, not the sumptuous delight to the senses it may be for some of us. She was very strict about her caloric consumption and when she went over 2000 calories on certain days, she scaled back her food intake that amount the following day. She openly admitted there were days she would prefer not to eat as much as she was supposed to, but she did.

When the day came for Patricia to leave for college, she did so, feeling proud, open, and happy. She left with the love and support of her parents and their acknowledgement that they had placed her in an unfair role and had been primarily responsible for her despair. She shared with them that she left with a little bit of guilt and fear knowing that they may well separate and/or divorce without her around to intervene. This was a very natural response for a child who was leaving without any certainty about what was going to happen to her parents after she left. Nonetheless, she went off to college, thus providing herself with the gift of a recovered life.

One might wonder: is this "real" recovery? After all, Patricia still holds rigid views regarding her eating, and she left her home feeling guilty and afraid while at the same time experiencing joy and pride at her entrance into college. With these mixed emotions and her "abnormal" view of food and eating, did Patricia actually recover?

For me, the answer is a resounding, "Yes!" Patricia made great strides in her relationship to her emotions and left her home without resuming her anorexic behaviors. She experienced the loss that comes with leaving her parents and had some fear about their relationship, but she didn't allow that to make her stay at home. The complexity of her emotions didn't drive her back to her anorexic behaviors. Her eating behavior wasn't what I would call ideal, but even if she maintained these habits and perceptions for the rest of her life, she could still have a full and very meaningful existence. She could develop friends, experience romantic relationships, engage in academic ventures, and have a successful career. Is there room to grow? Yes, of course. Might she benefit from more therapy in the future? Absolutely, but she now has the tools to decide on that path when and if she is ready. For Patricia, recovery meant being able to live her life again without the threat of losing everything to the eating disorder. Although she still thought a lot about food, she was able to enjoy life in ways that she had never dreamed of before. Most importantly, she opened up and had a real relationship with her emotional self. This is a real victory and a true recovery.

To get to this stage of recovery takes hard work on the part of the child and the parents. To achieve this you should continue using the exercises in this book as needed. It's not likely you will read through this book once, work the exercises, and magically your attachments to your child will be healed. You need to do the work outlined here consistently and, usually, over a long period of time before your child enters a consistent state of recovery and experiences fewer setbacks. As you do this work, trust that it is making a significant contribution to the resolution of your child's eating disorder.

As your child heals and engages less in her disturbed eating patterns, that doesn't mean your work is over. You need to make a lifelong commitment to maintaining a language of emotions and connecting with your child as you have over the course of this program.

In addition, you should keep working on providing your child with the space she needs to grow and analyzing some of your own underlying cultural beliefs that may have helped set the stage for the disorder to occur in the first place. By doing this you will deepen the healing process for yourself and your child. In the remainder of this chapter, I will offer some exercises that will help you do that, share some of my ideas on what it means to raise children in this culture, and explain what the eventual loss of the eating disorder means for you, your child, and your family.

Letting Go and Trusting in a Culture Opposed to Play

Can you remember what it was like to be curious as a young child — to be bold, creative, and to question or challenge? Do you remember what it was like not to care about how you looked or to feel that you always looked great or beautiful? Do you remember what it was like to have an imagination so vivid that you really believed that whatever you imagined was true?

These experiences are the essence of play, and play is the behavioral manifestation of true freedom. I believe freedom of this nature is woven into the very fabric of human existence. It's true that not all of us get to experience it as children. Due to the frailty of human character, some parents squash this sense of freedom in their children before it can become fully formed. If your own childhood was not marked with playful and carefree memories, this may have been true for you. Even so, you can consider how and why such play would be important to the emotional health and mental well-being of your child, and you can offer her the support she needs to experience real freedom in this very moment.

As important as symptomatic relief is when overcoming an eating disorder, the real jewel of recovery is the newfound freedom and sense of self your child discovers — the burgeoning autonomy we discussed in the last chapter. As she recovers, your child will develop a sense of who she is, what makes her tick, what she likes and dislikes, what she feels, and what she wants — and she will be able to express that to you. Through your empathy, you and she will develop a sense of safety and trust in each other. How great is that!

Hopefully both of you will be able to allow this creative process to unfold over time. Giving children the room to grow — the room to play and be free — does not generally mean providing them with the physical space to do this. Freedom, in the context of mental health, is about allowing your wishes and fantasies the room to breathe in your psyche. It's about exploring your reality and becoming who you most want to be. To do that you need to make space for play, creativity, and curiosity. You can offer this to your child by honoring her autonomy and respecting her voice, even if you don't always agree with what she says or the choices she makes. In fact, doing this is the greatest "food" you can provide her as she begins to recover, and she will need this if she is going to move forward without the danger of relapse. She will need to have your support to express the deep and authentic emotions she is beginning to experiment with. She will need you to emotionally hold her as she begins to play with her new life and try out new ideas and behaviors. If you and your child are going to heal, you must come to accept this as normal part of family life

Unfortunately, so much of the "freedom" we give our children stretches only as far as what fits in our culture's definition of what's acceptable. This is especially true when it comes to gender roles and body image. What would you think if your six-year-old daughter wanted to polish your two-year-old son's nails? How would you react if your four-year-old son marched proudly around your home with a pillow stuffed under his shirt declaring he was carrying a baby; or if your three-year-old daughter strutted around your home with a sock dangling from a string around her waist declaring, "Look at my penis!" Would you cringe if your six-year-old daughter was dancing in a ballet costume with her full belly exposed and draped over her tights? Perhaps some of these events, or some things very much like them, have already happened in your life. How did you respond?

If I'm pushing your buttons a bit here, that's good. I mean to! So many of our choices as parents are governed by societal expectations about gender roles instead of what is best for our children. Yes, there are studies that show that when little girls are put in a room with dolls and trucks they will more often choose to play with the dolls. Yes, little boys tend to play with the trucks. Certainly more research is needed regarding the degree to which nature versus nurture dictates behavior. The issue here is not whether boys choose trucks and girls choose dolls, but whether they are encouraged or discouraged one way or the other and how this kind of influence binds them inside gender roles that dictate their behavior as they mature. In other words, to what degree do we casually or specifically lead our children down paths that fit into what our culture expects from little girls and boys and ultimately from us as women and men?

Nowhere is this question more profound than in the area of body image and eating disorders. When we examine the role that culture and society play in the development of these illnesses, we find the influence is very strong. Eating disorders flourish in cultures where there are prescribed standards for what is desirable and beautiful regarding body size, shape, and attributes. For example, a study conducted in 1996 found that the amount of time adolescents spent watching soap operas and movies negatively influenced body image. The watching of music videos, in particular, was a predictive factor in the drive for thinness in youth. Interestingly, the total amount of television watched did not correlate with body dissatisfaction. It was these particular types of programs that influenced adolescents (Tiggemann and Pickering 1998). It would seem the quality of information consumed indeed influences our perceptions of ourselves.

Body dissatisfaction also thrives in cultures where expectations are placed on how girls and boys are supposed to look, think, feel, and/or behave. The idea that eating disorders are only associated with the upper levels of the socioeconomic ladder has been challenged. Though more research is needed, good studies are beginning to indicate that these disorders — especially bulimia nervosa and binge-eating disorder — may, in fact, be quite common in lower socioeconomic groups. The prevalence of eating disorders in cultures where women's behavior is highly restricted and where women have few choices beyond their role as wife and mother is inconsistent, but there are indications that this may play a role as well (Miller and Pumariega 2008). What all of this tells us is that cultural influences play a major role in the development of these problems.

Whether you are male or female, living in this culture means that messages regarding gender, beauty, and body shape are inescapable. We are bombarded with magazines and television shows and commercials whose messages about what is beautiful are strict, uncompromising, and totally unrealistic for most people. We are seduced by multi-billion-dollar beauty and diet industries, which manipulate us to buy more products that will enhance, improve, tighten, flatten, shrink, and reduce our bodies. We are all victims of this propaganda because we choose to listen and are convinced to believe. Some of us believe so much that we become convinced we must protect our children from stigmatization and teasing. We wouldn't want them to be "fat," for goodness' sake!

Obviously, parents have a responsibility to limit or restrict foods that lead to poor health. Saturated fats, sugar, chemicals, artificial sweeteners, and preservatives all fall in this category. The obesity epidemic in the United States is indeed real. It's also true these are the foods the diet industry teaches us lead to weight gain. But encouraging your children to eat whole and healthy foods is not the message that contributes to eating disorders. We all need to be eating a diet that is nutritionally balanced and represents *all* the food groups — including wonderful desserts!

The messages that pose a danger to our children are those we absorb from the media every day — those that promote thinness and beauty at any cost. What most don't realize is that a mere *one percent* of the population fits into what is portrayed as the "average" definition of female beauty in the media. Today we think nothing of hearing that yet another child star has developed anorexia or that the hottest new Hollywood actress drinks only lemon juice for 48 hours as part of a "detox fast" before every awards show. These are the messages that our children read and absorb every single day from one source or another. These are the messages that poison them with the idea that they must be "thin."

Many parents unconsciously support these social mandates for thinness at any cost. We want our children to fit in. We don't want them to be teased or stigmatized. Our greatest wish is to protect them. At first blush it looks like supporting your child's desire to be part of the culture makes sense. And in some ways it does. No one wants their child to be a pariah. But have you unwittingly bought into dangerous, unrealistic cultural messages in your desperation for your child to be accepted — messages that perpetuate our broken sense of what it means to be beautiful while lining a few powerful people's pockets with gold?

What's saddest about this pursuit for the idealized standard of beauty is that it is never attainable for most people. It's a lie perpetuated by the diet and beauty industries to convince us to buy their products. "You aren't quite thin enough or beautiful enough now, but if you try the next diet, purchase the next quick-fix beauty product, or buy clothing that is not designed to fit most teenagers (much less adults), maybe you'll get there." The diet and beauty industries will laugh all the way to the bank. These are the ideas they are feeding us and, sadly, we eat them up and serve them up to our children as well.

What would it be like to be free of them? What would it be like to offer your child the freedom to explore, to be creative, and to find her own place in our culture?

It is usually our fears that keep us constrained as parents. When our own preoccupation is with fitting in, we limit the degree to which we are able to allow our children to develop into fully mature, complete human beings. We put them in a kind of psychological prison built of the unanalyzed beliefs of our culture. Eating disorders signal this entrapment of mind, body, and spirit.

Yet, just as the eating disorder gives voice to pain, recovery gives voice to freedom, joy, and living an authentic life. Helping children with eating disorders grow against these cultural dictates is part of recovery. The joy in recovery comes in part from the freedom that is created by living in and loving *your* body. Can you support that new, freer voice in your child? Can you make changes in yourself and in your home that would establish an environment for that new voice to flourish? Here is an exercise that may help you do that.

Exercise: Challenging Feelings about Weight and the Body and Making Changes in Your Home to Support Recovery

Take out your journal once more and respond to these questions:

• Do you like your own body? What do you like about it? What don't you like about it?

- Does the reason you don't like a specific part or parts have to do with social and cultural stereotypes about what is beautiful and acceptable?
- Do you count calories, weigh yourself frequently, or obsess about your own body size and shape? What would it be like for you to give this up?
- Can you throw away the fashion and diet magazines in your home to provide your child some relief from their images?
- Do you spend time, money, and energy on dieting or researching the next new diet for yourself? Could you let go of dieting to model for your child a new resolve to confront and challenge the stereotypes of beauty that our culture cherishes?
- Can you talk in your home about what healthy eating means in a way that doesn't focus on weight or body?
- Do you avoid purchasing new clothing you need because you are waiting until you are the "right" size? What would it be like to go shopping with your child for clothes that fit no matter what sizes you and she are?
- Even if you have never voiced them, can you imagine how your own negative body image, negative self-assessment, and dissatisfaction might impact how your child learned to view her own body? Take a few moments to think about how your feelings about your own body may have influenced your child, and what you could do to change this.
- Are you obsessed with how your child's body looks? Do you concern yourself with making sure that your child fits into cultural and societal norms, regardless of whether your child's body is naturally slender or small-framed?

- Are you willing to no longer be "fat-phobic"? Do you know that eating fats does not make you fat and that eating healthy fats is vital to the maintenance of every organ system in the body, including the heart, brain, endocrine, skeletal, and reproductive systems?
- Can you look at your issues with your own body and challenge them, get help, and/or make food choices that are appropriate for your body as it is, consistent with needs due to age, health, body type, lifestyle, and the degree and type of exercise you engage in?
- Can you accept that your own body is unique?
- Can you accept that your child's body is unique?
- Can you understand how easy it is for your child to be influenced by messages in the media? Do you understand that she needs your voice to counter both these messages and the pressure she feels to conform?
- Do you understand that the standards for weight and beauty may have significantly changed since you were a teenager? That what is considered desirable now is unattainable for many people?
- Do you truly understand that your child is most influenced by how you behave, not by what you say? Do you practice what you preach?

This following exercise is for the person with an eating disorder.

Exercise: Understanding the Role of Cultural Messages about Weight and Body in Your Home and Family

Take out your journal and respond to the following:

- Do you think other people in your family like their own bodies?
- Do you think that your family is influenced by social and media messages regarding weight and body image?
- Do family members count calories, weigh themselves frequently, or obsess about their own body size and shape?

- Do your family members spend time, money, and energy on dieting or researching the next new diet?
- Does your family talk about what healthy eating means in your household in a way that doesn't focus on weight or body?
- Does anyone in your family avoid purchasing needed new clothing, because he or she waiting until he or she is the "right" size?
- Are members of your family obsessed with how your body looks and concern themselves with making sure that you fit into the cultural and societal norm, regardless of whether your body is naturally slender or small-boned?
- Are your family members "fat-phobic"? Do you think they know that eating fats does not make people fat and that eating healthy fats is vital to the maintenance of every organ system in the body, including the heart, brain, endocrine, skeletal, and reproductive systems?
- Do you think that your family members can look at their issues with their own body and challenge them, get help, and/or make food choices that are appropriate for the needs of their own body for their age, health, body type, lifestyle, and the degree and type of exercise they engage in?
- Do they accept that their own body is unique?
- Do they accept that your body is unique?
- Do you think that they understand how easy it is for you to be influenced by media messages?
- Do you think they understand that the standards for weight and beauty may have significantly changed since they were teenagers and that what is considered desirable now is unattainable for many people?
- Do you understand that you are more influenced by how your family behaves regarding weight, body image, and food than by what they say? Do they practice what they preach?

8
A Harmonious Life: Living in the Balance

Over the course of this book, I have attempted to help you peel away the proverbial layers of the onion of your child's eating disorder and the broken attachments and problematic family dynamics that led to it. An onion may seem like a strange metaphor to use, since it is a food, but I feel it is fitting. Food metaphors are some of the most visual and visceral in our language. That is one of the reasons your child used her relationship with food as a language to express what she could not say aloud.

If you have completed all or most of the exercises in this book, then you have an idea about what family factors contributed to the development of your child's eating disorder. You should now also understand why it is important that each member of your family accept responsibility for his or her contribution to that eating disorder, why emotional safety and trust are paramount in the creation of a healthy family infrastructure, why empathy is the key to a more connected and "attached" way of relating, and how to use a language of emotions to communicate honestly and openly with one another while still setting the appropriate boundaries your child needs to grow into a fully autonomous adult. This language of emotions can and will replace the language of food that each of you once relied on, either directly or indirectly, to express your needs and feelings toward each other. This language will help your child feel emotionally nourished by you. I hope you will continue to use the words you have learned to become increasingly more connected as a family.

Over time, your child will slowly learn to let go of the external voices that dictated her self-worth and self-esteem. Weight on the scale and other cultural expectations about what is desirable will become the outdated remnants of a punishing and self-defeating life. She will continue to learn that her internal voice is where true self-worth lives and she will begin to rely on that voice for wisdom and guidance. When she is ready to let go of the eating disorder, this voice will take its place. She will soon be able to consistently experience and express her emotions in an open and respectful way, and she will develop a sincere desire to take care of her body. In short, she will develop real self-worth based on her intrinsic value, not a false self-esteem based on her perceptions about the importance of having the perfect body or the perfect life.

As this happens, she may go through a period where she experiences grief over the loss of the eating disorder and the time and energy she put into it. Remember that, although unhealthy, when an eating disorder is functioning at its peak, it is a reliable, routine, dependable identity. It has been her best friend for years, and thus it makes sense that on some level she grieves its loss. Healing is, in part, about grieving what came before your child's eating disorder, the reasons her eating disorder arose, and the chaos, conflict, and disconnection that it created among your family. Her grief is a natural and necessary component of life and it is an important step in healing. We grieve because we have lost what or whom we have loved. Your child has lost much over the course of her disorder: The hours spent in the bathroom purging, the energy drained from her as she restricted calories, friendships or romantic relationships she may have lost along the way, the loss of her relationship with you. During her recovery she will eventually come to a place where she realizes she is about to lose the only thing she possessed during that awful period in her life — the disorder itself. Her grief for all these losses is very real.

Yet it is through this grief that she can be born anew into a life filled with more compassion and understanding about the human condition than many people may gain in a lifetime. Never forget that good mental health is about the integration of all negative and positive emotions — highly charged though they may be. Grief, loss, and anger certainly qualify and, by allowing herself to grieve, your child will slowly learn what it means to live in balance with all her emotions and lead a more harmonious life. Too often, people believe that to be healthy one must feel good all the time. This is not possible, nor is it even desirable. Powerful emotions like anger, sadness, shame, and grief are part of what makes us whole, healthy, and human. No life passes without these emotions. In fact, they aren't even "negative" when considered carefully. Feelings like these can impel the creative mind to write brilliant poetry, paint images that move us beyond words, and compose music that touches us so deeply that we listen over and over again. Through our grief, we learn to love again, often more tenderly and more effortlessly. How can any of this be considered "bad"?

As long as you respond to and reflect her voice back to her in an empathetic way, your child will be able to move through grief without relapse. Her trust in you and in the sense of safety you provide is the vessel that will carry her safely through. Once on the other side, she will start to encounter a newfound sense of freedom and a full reliance on her true self. She will learn to make choices that support her body, mind, and spirit. The days of self-recrimination will finally be at an end. And you will have contributed to that healing and that freedom.

This is the reward for families who engage in the process of recovery — they come away with the deeply gratifying knowledge that their hard work has led to better connections among family members and has offered their child an opportunity to heal in a deep and profound way.

You also receive the gift of feeling less on guard around your child. You can communicate in an open and authentic way. You can challenge and confront problems and behaviors while remaining empathetic and respectful. You no longer have to shield her from your feelings in the hopes of avoiding further problems, and you can finally depend on the fact that she realizes the disorder hurt you nearly as much as it did her. Your child isn't the only one who can enjoy the freedom that comes with recovery — you and the rest of your family get to partake, too!

As your child continues her journey to recovery, she will make peace with her disorder and the person who once needed its symptoms. You will make peace with it, too. Together you can use your newfound compassion to make family your most cherished "food" as you learn to emotionally nurture one another with greater sensitivity and love. Your child's eating disorder will then be transformed from curse to gift as you use the skills you learned from dealing with it to understand each other more deeply and to honor the frailty, vulnerability, and hope present in all human beings.

Appendix:
The Importance of Therapy

Many parents wonder at what stage they should seek therapy for their child with an eating disorder and what to look for in a therapist. While these questions are complex and an entire book could be written on this subject alone, in the pages that follow I would like to offer you some guidelines that may help you determine when it's time to seek professional help and what to look for when choosing a therapist.

When to Seek Help

Knowing when to seek treatment can be difficult, particularly when dealing with an adolescent. Body-image issues are part of an adolescent's task of identity formation, regardless of cultural messages, so it can be confusing to assess whether preoccupation with body image is normal or if your child has crossed over into something more serious like an eating disorder. The same is true for dieting. Many people diet, but not everyone who diets develops an eating disorder.

Certain conditions are obvious and are red flags that indicate you should seek therapy and medical intervention immediately. These include:

- Overt disordered eating behavior, such as purging, not eating for several days, obvious overeating, etc.

- Medical issues resulting from overt eating-disorder behavior, such as loss of menstruation, fainting, low energy, etc.
- A family member or your physician recommends you seek help.
- You feel you should seek help or your child asks to see a therapist.
- Your child experiences rapid weight loss.
- Dieting that does not stop despite achieving a healthy weight.
- Refusal to gain weight despite comments by concerned family members and friends.
- Dramatically limiting or ceasing to eat any food containing fats.
- Talking about a fear of eating food containing fat or carbohydrates.
- Your child has seen a nutritionist for a period of time without significant success regarding serious eating concerns.
- Your child is becoming increasingly agitated and/or depressed, is ruminating on appearance, or expresses feeling fat despite being a normal weight or less.
- Inability to engage in social and other activities.
- Your child cannot set parameters around food and is eating beyond what is healthy for body size and height and/or is eating in secret or in isolation.

Sometimes the signs that your child may have a problem that requires professional help are less obvious, and it can be very difficult to know what behaviors, thoughts, or moods should be taken seriously and evaluated professionally. For instance, if your child increasingly cuts back on certain foods, especially those containing fats, but maintains an appropriate weight, has a regular period, and is not vomiting, using laxatives to purge, or compulsively exercising, you may wonder whether it is advisable to seek professional help. Behaviors like these may indeed be indicative of a budding eating disorder, but that is not universally the case. To help you assess whether or not it is time to seek help, ask yourself the following questions:

- Does my child seem afraid to eat foods containing fat? (Note that there is a difference between resistance to eating fat and fear of these foods.)
- Does my child allow herself to eat a variety of foods without always knowing the exact ingredients?
- Is my child becoming more agitated, isolated, or depressed?
- Is my child obsessing over what she eats?
- Does my child seem to think about food a lot?
- Is my child frequently weighing herself?
- Does my child express fear of gaining weight or "being fat"?
- Is my child's mood or self-worth affected by the number on the scale or what she ate the day before?

If the answer to any of these questions is yes, first I recommend you discuss your concerns with your child. The simple reality is that you will not know how she feels or what she thinks about these issues unless you have a discussion. Families in which eating disorders arise often tend to avoid discussing the problem for fear of exacerbating the situation or hurting the child's feelings. In my view, this is a mistake. Not expressing your concern only serves to reinforce the denial and emotional avoidance that sets the stage for an eating disorder to flourish.

After discussing your concerns with your child, I suggest you consult with a therapist, and most certainly with a medical professional who can tell you whether or not your child is physically stable or in imminent danger. You and your child, if she is a minor, and in some cases as an adult, will need to be present during these consultations. Your child may protest against such intervention. Assuming that there are no outward signs that physical health or quality of life is in question, it may be difficult to convince her that her behavior could be problematic. For several reasons, I recommend that you pursue professional evaluation despite these protests.

A medical evaluation will determine whether or not her physical health is affected by her eating behavior. If it is, you have solid evidence that help is needed. If it isn't, this will allay some of your anxiety. Though a medical evaluation alone doesn't definitively determine whether or not your child has an eating disorder, it's an important step in understanding the severity of her potential problem.

Getting further evaluation from a licensed mental health practitioner who specializes in eating disorders will provide the additional insight you need to verify whether your concerns are justified. During this consultation, you will learn more about eating disorders, and you will begin to understand the issues surrounding them as they relate to your child. In the therapeutic environment you will have the opportunity to ask questions, address your concerns, and request advice about the need for treatment. If the therapist feels treatment is advisable, you can then ask questions about what to expect from treatment.

Even if treatment isn't necessary and the evaluations suggest that your child does not have an eating disorder, no harm can be done by seeking professional advice. In fact, by intervening with professional help, you show your child you care about her well-being and are attentive to her behaviors. What's more, it has often been my experience that even when a child outwardly protests a visit to a therapist, she is secretly relieved. She may well be concerned about her behavior and often has some questions of her own. Getting help and including your child in this process is usually a win-win situation.

However, if you are concerned that you may be overreacting or you are afraid to confront your child about these issues, you *can* seek the advice and recommendations of an eating-disorder specialist on your own before involving your child.

Whatever the case, when you seek the help of a therapist, there are a variety of things you will want to look for to make sure you are getting the help of someone who is fully qualified.

What to Look for in a Therapist

A therapist is someone who has been professionally trained to listen to you and help you make sense of the stories you tell, the feelings and thoughts you have, the beliefs you hold, and the motivations behind why you think and act in particular ways. When you enter into therapy, you enter into a relationship — a very profound relationship — that has a beginning and an end. Through this relationship, many truths are uncovered, insight and self-reflection is increased, feelings are expressed, and behavioral changes are made. In order for this to occur, particularly when dealing with individuals who have eating disorders, having a connection to the therapist is paramount. It is through this connection that a person can experience what lies underneath their eating disorder, confront the emotions that drive it, repair the relationships in their lives, and ultimately heal. The only way that is going to happen is if the person with the disorder comes to feel safe with, and trusts, the therapist.

While there are many things to take into consideration when choosing a therapist, including his or her theoretical approach, experience, and licensing, the most important is to find someone you and your child feel comfortable with and trust. Though everyone who enters therapy deserves to find someone he or she feels comfortable with, I believe that people with eating disorders, in particular, need empathetic therapists. Many people with eating disorders routinely feel different or strange — even crazy — because they equate having a negative feeling to "something being wrong with them." My approach fosters the idea that "we are in this together — therapist and patient," thus providing an openness to the experiences of my patients. And, since I view having an eating disorder as an adaptation to life that feels chaotic, stigmatization and judgment are removed. This results in a connection with another human being that helps them to learn — sometimes for the first time ever — that they are worthy of concern.

Though it is true that some patients with other psychological disorders actually benefit from a therapist maintaining an authoritative position, I discourage this approach with those who are struggling to heal from eating disorders because they are often vulnerable to authority. People with eating disorders typically fear authority figures, and often they will act out against authority, repeating patterns in the therapeutic relationship that mimic the feelings in the home or in other authoritative situations in which they felt threatened, afraid, or as though they were not nurtured and respected emotionally. I have seen too many cases where, as a result of an authoritative approach, the person with an eating disorder feels so intimidated that she simply stops coming for treatment. This does not mean that the therapist is without a voice that echoes of experience, competency, and expertise. It is this voice that allows for a good therapist to be challenging and simultaneously kind.

It has been my experience that people with eating disorders enter therapy afraid and hungry — hungry for an authentic voice of their own; hungry for someone to listen their stories; hungry for someone to understand their experiences; hungry for someone who does not think that they are crazy; and, perhaps most of all, hungry for someone to help them learn how to relate to other people. People with eating disorders often feel isolated and alone. If a therapist shows respect for the growing therapeutic relationship by remaining emotionally available, providing an environment conducive to the expression of feelings, and giving appropriate support and emotional nurturance, the process of recovery is less of a struggle.

Ultimately, you and your child have to decide what works best for you. Some therapists say more than others; some listen silently for long stretches of time; some ask more questions. Even people who practice in the same theoretical framework bring their individual experiences and personalities to bear on the way they practice. I recommend you take your time and find a therapist you can connect with. The relationship between the therapist and the client is often more important for the success of treatment than the theoretical approach taken. That means you should be sure to choose a therapist you feel you can trust. Most therapists offer the first session as a kind of "interview" to see whether you feel like the person is a good match for you. Take advantage of that, and don't hesitate to "interview" a few therapists before settling on one. Remember that trust takes time to develop and what you are looking for is a therapist who seems trustworthy.

During your first meeting, don't be afraid to ask the therapist about how he or she works, what his or her specialty is, what approach the person takes to eating disorders, or what he or she thinks the causes of eating disorders are. Question you might ask include:

- How long have you been treating eating disorders?
- How do you treat eating disorders?
- What is your philosophy about the cause of eating disorders?
- Do you work with physicians who treat the various medical conditions associated with eating disorders? If so, who?
- Do you work with a nutritionist who specializes in the treatment of eating disorders? If so, who?
- Do you have relationships with hospitals or residential treatment facilities so you can make a referral for more intensive care if the eating disorder gets worse?
- What age groups do you treat? Do you work with family members?

- What types of group treatments do you have for people with eating disorders and their family members?

By asking these questions, you should get a sense of the skill and qualifications of the clinician. By talking with him or her, you can determine whether you might be comfortable working with this person. If the therapist cannot answer your questions with confidence or if you do not feel comfortable conversing with the person, I advise you to look for someone else.

In addition to your sense of comfort and trust, there are a few things I recommend you focus on when searching for someone to help you and your child.

You will want to seek the assistance of a licensed professional who specializes in, and is seasoned in, the treatment of eating disorders. If your child were sick with cancer, you would send her to an oncologist, not a cardiologist. You can think about therapy the same way. There are many therapists out there that have a basic understanding of eating disorders. You want to find a person who specializes in them and understands the specific psychological underpinnings that contribute to these problems. Watch out for therapists who are jacks-of-all-trades but masters of none. Several websites are listed in the Resource section of this book where you can access names of specialists in your area who treat eating disorders. You may also ask your primary health care professional for a recommendation. Many primary care providers have relationships with eating-disorders specialists to whom they refer patients.

During the initial assessment period, your therapist should ask questions, even if he or she is typically the silent type. There is quite a bit a therapist needs to know when assessing someone with an eating disorder. A therapist who fails to properly investigate the history of the problem is someone you likely will want to shy away from.

All mental health clinicians specializing in eating disorders should have physicians to whom they refer their clients for medical care and follow-up. This is an essential point. If the therapist you are meeting with does not have these kinds of affiliations, stay away. No patient with an eating disorder should be treated without the possibility of timely medical evaluation and care. That doesn't mean you *have* to see the medical professional the therapist recommends. You and/or your child may already have a good relationship with your family's primary care provider, and if he or she is comfortable treating the medical issues associated with eating disorders, a good therapist will not discourage this. In any event, the therapist you choose should have connections with and be comfortable interfacing with medical professionals. He or she will need to collaborate and communicate with your child's doctor during the course of therapy. The medical provider will determine the frequency of medical visits and the medical care administered.

Today, many therapists, me included, treat eating disorders by using an integrative model that includes the services of a registered dietician or nutritionist. I have found that utilizing a nutritionist in the recovery process is of vital importance in sound care. A good nutritionist who has an understand of eating disorders can help support many of the behavioral changes that need to happen regarding food and the body, and can help your child set goals to reduce or eliminate symptoms, find alternatives to bingeing and purging, identify emotional or relational triggers which lead to symptomatology, and suggest alternatives to "trigger" foods. Nutritionists also teach about the body's metabolism, physiology, processing of food and calories, and how to distinguish "stomach" hunger from "mouth" or "emotional" hunger. All of this serves as an incredibly important adjunct to therapy, and I encourage you to find a therapist who works in collaboration with a nutritionist. That said, nutritionists are not therapists. No nutritionist should ever claim that she can treat the psychological aspects of an eating disorder unless she is also a licensed mental health professional. Nutritional care should be finite and generally shorter-term than therapy. Frequency of visits, though initially fairly often, should decrease over time.

Most therapists practice within a particular theoretical psychological framework, and there are many such, including psychodynamic therapies (which have a variety of subcategories), cognitive-behavioral therapy (CBT), family therapy, dialectical behavioral therapy (DBT), psychoanalysis, behavioral therapy, medication therapy, and expressive therapies (including art, drama, experiential, and movement). Most reputable eating-disorder specialists are familiar with the principles of all of these therapies and utilize a combination of them in treatment. Generally, however, most therapists orient their approach primarily toward one or two of these frameworks. Each framework offers its own explanation(s) regarding human development, individual behavior, issues, problems, and disorders. A therapist is trained to listen, observe, and interpret a person's words and behavior in the context of the framework under which he or she practices.

This means that different psychological models have different explanations for how eating disorders develop and what recovery means. For instance, traditional psychological models, such as psychodynamic therapies or psychoanalysis, believe a "cure" is created when the person with an eating disorder obtains a deep understanding of what caused the disorder, makes efforts to repair and heal relationships affected by it, and learns to live life authentically and honestly. The "cure" is created because the symptoms are no longer necessary and because the purpose that the eating disorder served has been replaced by what is real and sustaining in life.

Cognitive-behavioral models, on the other hand, target irrational beliefs and self-destructive behaviors and focus on altering thinking, challenging beliefs, improving problem-solving, providing education and relapse-prevention strategies, and providing alternatives to self-destructive behavior. Recovery is measured by goals reached, symptoms reduced or eliminated, and weight restoration.

A commonality I have found between these two seemingly disparate models is that they both work toward helping people learn to sit with and experience their negative and highly charged emotional states without resorting to eating-disorder behaviors to calm, soothe, mask, control, or deflect the intensity of their emotions. Sitting with emotion and allowing for the process of discovery are goals of recovery, regardless of the theoretical orientation.

I believe it is impossible to recover from an eating disorder without doing both the behavioral work necessary to change problematic eating patterns and addressing the underlying relational and emotional issues that form the deep root of the psychological difficulties on which these problematic behaviors are founded. For this reason, I use a combination of a solid psychodynamic model (focusing on insight, identifying and expressing emotions, understanding the motivations behind the eating disorder, building new relationships, and healing and strengthening current ones) and cognitive-behavioral treatment methods that deal with the immediate behavioral problems necessary for sustaining health and quality of life. In my view this makes for a strong "cocktail" for recovery, and I have used it successfully with many, many patients.

While effective, reliable, and scientifically sound, I have found that using a cognitive-behavioral model alone can lead to understanding recovery as the elimination of a bad habit or a focus that relies solely on the social and media messages your child has latched onto. In my view true recovery from an eating disorder must involve helping the person understand her internal psychological world, recognize what the eating disorder has been a representation for in her life, and rethink the way she relates to herself, the people around her, and the world at large. It should reflect a positive change in how she perceives herself and how she perceives herself in relation to others. I have found the attachment model that this book is based on is the best theoretical framework for achieving these goals.

Whomever you eventually choose to help your child and your family, I would encourage you to consider seeking the help of someone who is as invested in addressing the deep roots of the condition as I am. Healing the underlying emotional trauma and family dynamics that drive disorders of this nature can lead to deep and profound changes that serve as the foundation for lifelong health and happiness.

Resources

The following is a list of inpatient and residential treatment facilities Cedar Associates has worked with over the years. Each facility has provided valued care to some of our patients for which we are extremely grateful. There are many other excellent inpatient treatment facilities available. At the end of this list are websites that list others, as well as websites to find outpatient programs and individual, family, or group outpatient treatment providers.

The Renfrew Center, the country's first residential eating disorder treatment facility. Specializing solely in the treatment of anorexia, bulimia, and binge eating disorder, its innovative programs emphasize the value and healing potential of healthy relationships. renfrewcenter.com (Pennsylvania and Florida)

The Meadows, America's leading treatment center for addiction and trauma. The Meadows is based on the 12-Step model and traditions of healing and trauma resolution. themeadows.org (Arizona and Texas)

Oliver Pyatt Centers, comprehensive treatment program for women with anorexia, bulimia, binge eating disorder, and exercise addiction. oliverpyattcenters.com (Florida)

Avalon Hills Eating Disorder Treatment Center, assisting adolescents as well as adults in altering the negative beliefs, emotions, behaviors, interactions, and cultural influences that have contributed to the development of disordered eating. avalonhills.org (Utah)

Columbia Center for Eating Disorders, an internationally recognized program with nearly thirty years of commitment to the research and treatment of eating disorders.
Columbiacenterforeatingdisorders.org (New York)

Timberline Knolls, one of the leading residential treatment centers in the U.S. Helps women struggling with eating disorders, alcohol abuse, co-occurring disorders, drug addiction, mood disorders, and trauma. www.timberlineknolls.com (Illinois)

Websites to explore when searching for a residential facility or qualified outpatient eating disorder therapist in your community.

Academy for Eating Disorders, a global professional association committed to leadership in eating disorders research, education, treatment, and prevention. www.aedweb.org

National Eating Disorders Association (NEDA), supports individuals and families affected by eating disorders and serves as a catalyst for prevention, cures, and access to quality care. www.nationaleatingdisorders.org

Eating Disorders — Gürze Books, a bookstore of over 300 hand-picked titles, hundreds of articles, a therapist directory, and listings of national organizations and treatment centers. www.bulimia.com

Eating Disorders Referral and Information Center, comprehensive database of anorexia, bulimia, and other eating disorder professionals. www.edreferral.com

References

Brumberg, J. 2000. *Fasting Girls: The History of Anorexia Nervosa.* New York: Vintage.

Kaminker, L. 1998. *Exercise Addiction: When Fitness Becomes an Obsession.* New York: The Rosen Group.

Miller, M. N. and Pumariega, A. 2008. Eating disorders: Culture and eating disorders. http://www.healthyplace.com/eating-disorders/main/eating-disorders-culture-and-eating-disorders/menu-id-58/

Sullivan, P. 1995. Mortality in anorexia nervosa. *American Journal of Psychiatry, 152*(7), 1073-1074.

Tiggemann, M. and Pickering, A. 1998. Role of television in adolescent women's body dissatisfaction and drive for thinness. *International Journal of Eating Disorders. 20*(2): 199–203.

About the Author

Judy Scheel, Ph.D., LCSW, has been treating eating disorders for more than 25 years integrating psychodynamic theory and cognitive treatment strategies in her work. During her years providing treatment she has formulated and strengthened her beliefs that mutual respect, empathy, and trust between patient, family, and therapist are second to none in providing the foundation for familial and relational repair and recovery from an eating disorder. Helping patients live authentically remains the cornerstone of her approach to treatment.

Dr. Scheel is the Founder and Executive Director of Cedar Associates, a private outpatient program, founded in 1994 and located in Westchester County, NY, specializing in the treatment of eating disorders and other self-harm behaviors. Cedar Associates is currently conducting research on the role of the therapeutic relationship in eating disorder recovery. She is the President of Cedar Associates Foundation, Inc., a not-for-profit organization dedicated to eating disorder prevention, education, and research.

Dr. Scheel has co-produced a nationally distributed educational video with teaching manual for students in grades 8-12 on eating disorders and prevention.

She has been a lecturer at Purchase College, SUNY and a frequent presenter at local, regional, and national conferences. She writes for online and print newsletters. She is a member of the National Eating Disorders Association (NEDA), Academy for Eating Disorders (AED), and the Eating Disorders Coalition, Inc., a public policy organization in Washington, DC.

Dr. Scheel has a daughter and son, two shelter dogs and lives in NYC with practices in NYC and Westchester. She is an avid international traveler and loves to run in the rain and ride her bicycle around NYC.